Endorsemen

An entertaining and unusua
and sensitive four-year-old. I ... unexpected
insights for parents.

—Dr. Tom Phelan
Author of the best-selling book
1-2-3 Magic: Effective Discipline for Children 2-12

It has been said that the best way to get a young child's perspective is to get down on your knees and crawl, taking in the sights from his or her eye level. That is exactly what Rob Currie does in this book. As a parent and new grandparent, I can appreciate the reminder to look into the heart of a child to truly understand his or her actions and words. Rob's insight into a child's mind helps us to communicate with our children more effectively. It's a must-read for parents and grandparents!

—Jeanie Fields
Sr. Director at Hearts at Home

Rob Currie uses his unique humor and wit to teach parents practical life and parenting lessons. He will clearly make you laugh, but more importantly, he will challenge your parental thinking.

—Tom Bienert
Children's Pastor Willow Creek Community Church

There's a theologian inside of every child, as this psychologist wisely illustrates. His stories also remind us that "little potatoes have big eyes."

—Paula Spencer
Coauthor of the best-selling book, *The Happiest Toddler on the Block,* and author of *Momfidence: An Oreo Never Killed Anybody and Other Secrets of Happier Parenting*

With a clever and unique approach, Currie pulls us into a preschooler's world and reminds us of simple, yet profound truths of child thinking and feeling—truths that will greatly aid with the challenges of day-to-day child rearing.

—Karin R. Anderson, Ph.D.
Assistant Professor of Psychology and Counselor Education Concordia University Chicago

Lori is a very perceptive young child. She gets to the heart of things and makes sensible connections between motives and actions. It's a good thing that Rob Currie overheard some of her humorous conversations and recorded them for us.

—Roger Schmurr
Editor of *Christian Home and School*

As a grandmother of six "young theologians," I warmed to the lessons that Lori teaches. What a clever and amusing way to have our grandparenting and parenting skills examined and honed! *This is a wonderful gift for parents and grandparents.*

—Jane Patete
Women's Ministries Coordinator Presbyterian Church in America

For over twenty years, in his teaching, writing, and presentations, Dr. Currie has demonstrated a gift for bringing psychological theories and findings to bear on practical concerns. He creatively uses a precocious four-year-old to help us better understand how children think and feel. A delightful read, yet full of instructive and practical insights.

—Wayne Joosse, Ph.D.
Professor of Psychology Emeritus, Calvin College

This book will make you smile, laugh, and see life through the eyes of a child…again.

—Mark Lowry
Christian Comedian

This is a very enjoyable and helpful book. Dr. Currie channels his instructional gifts through the eyes of a preschooler and reminds us of the importance of perspective, clarity, patience, and values when caring for our little ones.

—Steven C. Guy, Ph.D.
Pediatric Neuropsychologist Columbus, OH

Dr. Currie is a gifted teacher and storyteller. He distills the essence of childhood into principles even an adult can understand! *Preschool Wisdom* approaches meaningful lessons and shares them in ways that make them a delightful read. As a big sister, I'd recommend sharing this with the entire family.

—Cheryl L. Richter
Christian Author and CPA

Preschool Wisdom

Preschool Wisdom

What Preschoolers Desperately Want to Tell Parents and Grandparents

Rob Currie, Ph.D.

Published by Redemption Press, PO Box 427, Enumclaw, WA 98022.

ISBN 13: 978-1-63232-742-0

Library of Congress Catalog Card Number: 2010904853

Special Notice

Note to the Reader

To get more out of this book, recruit a few friends to read and discuss it with you. Use the discussion questions after each chapter to cement the ideas in your mind, to learn practical tips from others, and to enjoy conversation with others who are parents or grandparents of preschoolers. I also encourage you to visit the Web site— Ilovemypreschooler.com.

This book is dedicated with love to:

My parents, Ken and Ferne Currie, for being an example of a loving marriage; my wife, Kay Currie, for being my bride and joy; and to our sons, Sam and Steven Currie, for being fine young men.

Special thanks go to:

Christy Ascheman, Mona Ballard, Pat Hargis, Janet Riehecky, Les Stobbe, and Renee Werner for making this book possible.

Contents

1. The Cookie Principle 1
2. Scaredy-cat 5
3. Big Deal 9
4. Don't Forget 13
5. Grown-ups Say the Darndest Things 17
6. Does Grandpa Know Why? 21
7. Oh No! 25
8. Guess What I Saw 29
9. Look What I Found 33
10. Heigh-ho, Heigh-ho 37
11. Yippee! 41
12. What Makes Mommy Smile 45
13. When Are We Going to Be There? 49
14. No, It Isn't! 53
15. A Dumb Day 57
16. Help Me 61
17. The Big Purchase 65
18. Uh-Oh 69
19. Yummy! 73
20. The Bride and the Goon 77
21. Grandpa's Secret 81
22. No Grandma and Grandpa 85

23. Will Grandpa Be OK? 89
24. When Grandma Reads to Me 93
25. Guess Who 97
26. The Race 101
27. The Gift 105

Endnotes 109

Deleted Scenes 111

Recommended Resources 115

Ten Quick Tips for Parents of Preschoolers 117

Ten Quick Tips for Grandparents of Preschoolers 119

Author Interview 121

You May Have a Preschooler if... 123

Topical Index 125

"We are most alive and ready for transformation when we learn to listen to our children, and it's never too late to learn."[1]

Dan Allender
How Children Raise Parents

"A little 'un can sometimes see things in others that us older ones cannot because our judgment gets clouded."[2]

Brian Jacques
The Bellmaker

Every Tuesday evening, Grandpa and Grandma come over to babysit Lori, who is four years old, and her baby brother, Tommy. During their visit, Lori talks to Tommy.

Chapter 1

The Cookie Principle

Tuesday, March 2nd

HI, TOMMY, THIS is Lori. You know, your big sister. Since you're only two months old and I'm four years old, I'm going to explain some stuff to you about kids and grown-ups. These are things you need to understand, 'cause if you do, your life will be way better. I know what it's like for you. I used to be little too.

See, there's all kinds of real important stuff you need to know about being a kid and what kids are like. I'm going to tell you 'cause Mommy and Daddy can't. They used to know it when they were kids, but they've forgotten it all 'cause it's been so long since they were little. But don't worry, little brother. I'll explain it all to you. But you have to listen, O.K.?

The first thing you need to know is that grown-ups can't make up their minds. First they want one thing and then another. They can't decide, 'cause they don't know what they want. I know what I want. I want a cookie, but Mommy said, "No, how about a banana?" She said, "A cookie will ruin your appetite for dinner." But I don't want dinner, 'cause it'll ruin my appetite for a cookie. And I don't want a banana; I want a cookie.

You see, grown-ups are always trying to get us kids to do stuff we don't want to do. They make us try different foods we don't like, and if we want to watch TV, they tell us to color or play a game. We know what we want, but they keep trying to get us to like other stuff. By the time we get to be Mommy and Daddy's age, we won't know what we want anymore. But I'm a kid, and I know what I want. Do I want to go to bed? No. Do I want a cookie? Yes.

I feel sorry for Mommy and Daddy 'cause they don't know what they want. They can't help it. They're grown-ups. They can't decide whether to leave the toilet seat up or down. Daddy wants it up, but Mommy wants it down. They were talking real loud about it today. I asked, "Why are you arguing?" Daddy said, "We're not arguing. We're discussing." After they were done, I snuck in the bathroom and put the toilet seat back up so I could hear them discuss it again.

Another thing they can't decide is whether or not they want to move to a different town. They should just listen to me 'cause I'm a kid, and it's easy for me to decide stuff. I don't want to move 'cause I really like living here in St. Louis. I like being close to Grandma and Grandpa, I like our house, and I like being next door to my best friend, Sarah.

But Mommy and Daddy don't know what they want. Mommy doesn't know what she wants to fix for dinner. I told her, "You should fix cookies." She said no. In the morning, she can't decide what she wants to wear. Sometimes Daddy asks her, "What do you want to do on Saturday?" She usually says, "I don't know."

Daddy is just as bad. He can't decide what to watch on TV. He sits in his chair with his remote control and changes channels all the time. He doesn't know what he wants to watch 'cause he's been a grown-up too long. I bet when he was a kid he wanted to watch lots of cartoons on TV, but his parents made him watch other shows. And I bet when he was little, he wanted cookies real bad, but his parents made him eat a bunch of different stuff. Now he doesn't know what he wants.

Tommy, I've got lots of important things to tell you. I sure wish grown-ups remembered this stuff from when they were kids, 'cause if they did, they'd be awesome parents and grandparents. But since they don't, I'll explain it all to you.

Anyway, Daddy doesn't even know which job he wants. Somebody offered him a job in Detroit. That's why we might move. He is thinking about changing jobs, but it's hard for him to decide. So Daddy listened to a CD about how to be a success. I heard part of the CD. The man on the CD said if you want to be a success, you have to figure out what you want and go after it. That means I'm going to be a real big success 'cause I know what I want. I really want a cookie.

When the CD was over, Mommy sat next to Daddy, held his hand, and asked him, "Which job do you really want?" He looked down at the floor and didn't say anything for a long time. Then he lifted his head, looked at Mommy, and said, "I don't know." So Mommy hugged him. I hugged him too. And I gave him a cookie.

TAKE-AWAY VALUE

Think About It

Preschool children are charming and challenging, in part because they think very differently than adults. In this book, you'll learn how the disparity between your viewpoint and your child's impacts areas such as rule-making, bedtime, mealtime, story time, playtime, addressing fear, resolving arguments, emotional struggles, chores, discipline, shopping, and more. You'll understand how your child perceives these issues, and you'll learn simple and practical responses that really work. As you do, you'll get a happier and more obedient child. In addition, you'll enjoy him or her more than you thought possible.

Talk About It

1. Describe a time when you were frustrated because someone misunderstood you.
2. How did that make you feel toward that person?
3. Relate an instance where someone understood you really well. How did that make you feel toward that person? Did it help you cope with your feelings?
4. How will your child feel when you understand him or her much better?

Try It

If you haven't already, ask a friend or two to read the book and discuss it with you.

Chapter 2

Scaredy-cat

Tuesday, March 9th

GRANDPA AND GRANDMA just got to our house. They come over to babysit us every Tuesday while Mommy and Daddy go out. But Mommy and Daddy are talking to Grandma and Grandpa right now. And before our grandparents babysit us tonight, I have to ask you something, Tommy. Have you ever been scared?

This morning, Mommy said, "Let's go, Lorikins. It's time to go to the dentist." But I ran and hid under my bed 'cause Teddy Bear was scared the dentist would hurt me. When she said, "Lori Alexis Griffin, come here right now!" I knew she was mad 'cause she was using my middle name. You know you're in trouble when Daddy or Mommy calls you by your middle name. When I take Mommy's special necklace and play with it without asking, she hollers, "Lori Alexis Griffin! Don't take my necklace!"

Grown-ups want our middle names to be special to us, but they ruin everything by using our middle names only when they're angry at us. Sheesh! But when Jesus was born, God knew Jesus wouldn't get in any trouble. So God didn't give him a middle name, just a first name and a last name. He just named him "Jesus Christ."

Anyway, I was hiding under the bed, and Mommy didn't know where I was. Then Teddy Bear said, "If you stay under the bed, maybe Mommy will never find you. Then she'll be sad and cry a lot."

Then I started thinking. If Mommy couldn't find me, she might get so lonely she'd invite some other girl to our house just to have someone to play with. Mommy and Daddy would take her to play in Tower Grove

Park, and afterwards, they'd drive to Ted Drewes for frozen custard and buy *her* some instead of *me*. So I stuck one foot out from under the bed so Mommy could find me.

When she found me, she was mad at me for hiding. So I told her, "Teddy is scared the dentist will hurt me." She said, "The dentist is a nice man, and he'll help take care of your teeth." I told her, "Teddy is still scared, and he wants you to tell the dentist to be nice." Mommy said, "The dentist is very nice, and you may take Teddy Bear with you and hold him while the dentist checks your teeth."

When we got to the dentist, Mommy told him, "My daughter is a little frightened." I said, "I'm not scared, but Teddy Bear is worried I'll get hurt." The dentist smiled and said, "Your Teddy Bear sounds very nice." Then the dentist put Teddy Bear in the chair and showed how he would check and clean my teeth. Teddy liked the part when the chair moved up and down. When the dentist finished with Teddy, he helped Teddy Bear pick a toy from the toy chest for being brave, but Teddy said he wanted me to have it.

Then the dentist told me, "Lori, now you get a turn in the special chair." I held Teddy Bear, and Mommy watched. And you know what? Mommy was right. The dentist was nice. He was very gentle when he cleaned my teeth, and when he finished, he said, "You may have another toy for being so good." So I picked out a toy. Then I told the dentist, "You can choose a toy 'cause you were so nice."

He asked me what kind of food I like. I told him, "I like cookies." He said, "I want you to eat healthy food so your teeth will be strong." I told him, "I'll eat lots of healthy food and lots of cookies."

When we got back from the dentist, Mommy took us for a walk. My friend Sarah and her mommy were walking their dog. Do you remember, Tommy? You were in the stroller, and you cried when the dog barked. You were scared, weren't you? You don't have to be scared of that dog. He's nice. And you don't have to be scared of the dentist 'cause you don't have any teeth.

I know what you were scared of. You were scared that our family might move away from St. Louis. I'm scared of that too. If we move, we'll barely ever get to see Grandma and Grandpa. I'll miss sitting on Grandma's lap when she reads to me; I'll miss Grandpa telling me a story when he tucks me in bed on Tuesday nights; and I'll miss my friend Sarah, who lives next door.

But I know how to fix this whole thing, Tommy. I'll tell Grandma and Grandpa to tell Mommy that we shouldn't move. She's their daughter, and she has to obey them. And I'll put a Bible on the dining room table so she won't forget what the Bible says about obeying her parents.

Being scared is real hard for us kids, and even though Mommy and Daddy are nice, sometimes they forget how hard it is when we're afraid. So when I get scared, they tell me, "Your nightmare wasn't real, and the scary noise you heard wasn't anything bad." Or they tell me, "You don't have to be afraid of moving." They forget that when kids are scared, we really just want a hug. When Mommy hugs me, it feels like she's way bigger than anything I'm scared of, and that helps me feel better. And I don't like it when grown-ups keep saying, "There's nothing to be afraid of," 'cause that just means they don't understand how scared I am.

Sometimes when you get scared, I let you hold Teddy Bear, and you stop crying. But you'd better ask Mommy for your own Teddy Bear, 'cause when we both get scared I'm going to hug him 'cause he's mine.

So don't be a scaredy-cat, Tommy. You should be brave like Grandpa. We called him on the phone, and I told him about my trip to the dentist. He said he's going to the dentist to get a fruit canal. So I told Grandpa, "Be real good for the dentist, and he'll let you choose a toy when you're done." Grandpa said, "That's a good idea." And I told him, "You can borrow Teddy Bear." He said, "Thank you, but I won't need a Teddy Bear, 'cause I've got Grandma."

I'm not brave like Grandpa yet, so I'll keep hugging Teddy Bear when I get scared. And Teddy Bear needs me, too. He needs me to play with him and to hug him when he's scared.

TAKE-AWAY VALUE

Think About It

Have you ever tried bumper bowling? That's when the bowling alley puts rails on either side of a bowling lane, so a bad throw won't go in the gutter. The rails redirect the ball to hit the pins.

When Lori was afraid, rather than offering criticism, her mother and the dentist gently steered her thoughts toward Teddy Bear and the dentist's special chair. When your child experiences fear , acknowledge his or her feelings. Then redirect the child's attention. For example, "You're right. Going to preschool is a new experience. Which playground toys will you want to play with there?" Or, "That's true; we might see some bugs when we go camping. Do you think you'll have more fun hiking or swimming?" Or, "Yes, it's dark in the bedroom. Do you want to sleep with a stuffed animal?"

Talk About It

1. What frightened you as a child?
2. When someone belittles your concerns, how does that make you feel?
3. What concerns do your children express?
4. How do you gently redirect your child's thoughts and behavior?

Try It

Pick a concern your child expresses and choose a way to steer his or her thoughts to something more pleasant.

Chapter 3

Big Deal

Tuesday, March 16th

PSST! TOMMY! ARE you awake? Good, 'cause there's something kind of strange about grown-ups. They really like big stuff.

When we eat out, Daddy likes a big glass of soda pop, and Mommy likes a big cup of coffee. Our parents like to take us for walks in Forest Park 'cause it's really big. Grown-ups like big stuff at work, too. Daddy said, "This deal is very important. It's the biggest deal I've ever worked on." See what I mean? Grown-ups like big stuff .

I bet that's why they want to move. Daddy wants a bigger job, and Mommy wants a bigger house. And they want to move to a bigger town.

I don't want to move! But the real estate lady is coming to ask Mommy and Daddy if they want to sell our house and move. I'll try to talk Mommy and Daddy out of moving, and you can help too, Tommy. When that lady comes, you have to scream and cry. Then our parents will know you don't want to move either, and they'll change their minds.

I like some big things, like cookies and stuff. But grown-ups like a lot of big things. And they like big people too 'cause big people are more important than little people. So grown-ups get to tell kids what to do since they're larger than us. And Mommy says I can't cross the street by myself until I'm bigger. I told her, "I *am* bigger. I'm four years old!" But she said I have to get even bigger. Sheesh!

And in the car, big people like Mommy and Daddy get to sit in front by the radio. But you and I have to sit in the back 'cause we're littler. We have special seats in the back seat, but the big people in front get seat belts *and* big bags that fill up with air real fast if we crash into something.

We're too little to sit in the front 'cause in an accident, we'd get smooshed by the two windbags in the front seat.

You can tell grown-ups like big stuff and big people by the way they talk to kids. When grown-ups want to make us feel special, they tell us we're big. Today at the store, we saw Mrs. Watson from church. She looked at you and said, "Hi, sweetheart." (That's what grown-ups call you when they don't remember your name.) She said, "You are both getting so big." I told her, "Thank you. You are getting really big, too." Then Mommy bit her lip and tried not to laugh, but I don't know why.

Here's another thing about grown-ups liking big stuff. They say presents aren't the most important part of Christmas. But they don't mean it. They put up a tree in the living room that's as big as Daddy, and they spend the whole evening decorating it with big ornaments and lights. Then they open a box and pull out a manger that's so little it fits on my lap. If the presents aren't as important as Jesus being born, then how come the tree is so much bigger than the manger?

And there's something else kind of funny about grown-ups liking big stuff. In Sunday school, our teacher helped us learn Matthew 6:19 . It says, "Do not store up for yourselves treasures on earth..."[3] She said "treasure" is another word for getting more stuff and bigger stuff. But Tommy, it sure seems like grown-ups try hard to get a lot more stuff and bigger stuff. I guess they haven't learned that verse in their Sunday school class yet.

Here's another thing about being big. I asked Mommy one time, "Why does God get to be God instead of somebody else being God?" She said, "That's a good question." (That's what grown-ups say when they don't know the answer.) She said, "I can't explain it, but I'm glad he's God."

Mommy doesn't know, but I figgered it out. (I told you I was going to explain this stuff to you.) God gets to be God 'cause he's bigger than everybody. He is so big he can help everybody in the whole world and not get tired even if it's way past bedtime. And he does a good job 'cause he's been God for a long time, and he's had lots of practice.

So remember, Tommy, grown-ups like big stuff. That's why our parents want to move. Don't forget what I told you. When that real estate lady comes tomorrow, you have to scream and cry. O.K.? Good. And remember to eat your food and keep growing 'cause then you'll get big and people will be nice to you. O.K., Tommy?

Grandma and Grandpa are babysitting us. They do that every Tuesday night. They're going to put us to bed soon, but since grown-ups like big stuff, tonight I'm going to stay awake until Mommy and Daddy come home, so I can give them a hug. A GREAT BIG one.

TAKE-AWAY VALUE

Think About It

Lori points out adults' fascination with big things. Her comments illustrate the fact that in the process of raising our preschoolers, we learn to see ourselves in new ways.

This is important because training our kids is just one side of being a good parent or grandparent. The other side requires you to learn and grow, often as a result of your interaction with your youngster. The fact that you are more mature than your preschooler should not keep you from recognizing your need to continue to improve and change. Novelist Peter DeVries understood this. He wrote , "For who of us is mature enough for offspring before the offspring themselves arrive? The principle of society is forced growth. The value of marriage is not that adults produce children but that children produce adults."[4]

Talk About It

1. Have you known a person who refused to change to meet someone else's needs?
2. How did that make you feel?
3. How have you changed as a result of being a parent or grandparent? How has that helped you in your relationship with your preschooler?
4. If your child could change one reasonable thing about the way you relate to him or her, what would it be?

Try It

Tell someone what you're learning from your relationship with your child or grandchild.

Chapter 4

Don't Forget

Tuesday, March 23rd

LISTEN UP, LITTLE brother. I don't have much time to talk, so I'm going to talk fast. It's bedtime, and I'm supposed to be putting on my jammies. Grandma's in the bathroom, and Grandpa's watching a little bit of his favorite movie, *Saving Private Meg Ryan*.

Remember I told you that the real estate lady was coming to our house? I have some really bad news about that. And, oh...Grandma's out of the bathroom, and now she's in the kitchen washing dishes and watching us. So when she leaves the kitchen, I'll tell you more about the real estate lady and my secret plan to keep us from moving. But first, I'll tell you something else.

You are going to be seeing Mommy and Daddy a lot, so you need to know that they're very nice, but they forget stuff. Since you were born, they've forgotten when to sleep. I hear them talk about getting up a lot at night, and I see them taking naps during the day. I think they have their days and nights mixed up.

Parents lose stuff 'cause they forget where they put it. Mommy forgets where she puts your pacifier. She teases Daddy and tells him he has a pacifier too, but it's called a TV remote control. Daddy smiles and says Mommy's pacifier is a cup of coffee.

Sometimes they lose important stuff. One time, Mommy said, "I'm losing my mind." Yesterday, Daddy lost you. He was playing peek-a-boo with you. He put a blanket over your crib and said, "Where's Tommy? Where's my boy?" I had to tell Daddy, "He's right there, under the blanket!"

Parents forget stuff on long car trips. They forget that time goes real slow for kids. So when we drive to a vacation, I ask, "When are we going to be there?" Mommy says, "It only takes four hours to get to Uncle John's house." But it feels like forever. And grown-ups say, "Wow, this year went by in a hurry!" But kids don't say that 'cause time goes way slower for us.

Grown-ups forget lots of things. Mommy wears makeup, but I think she forgets that pretty isn't something you put on from the outside. Her pretties are on the inside, and they come out when she smiles. Daddy's good looks are on the inside too, and they come out when he laughs. When he has a hard day, his good looks get smooshed way down inside and take longer to come out. And Mommy and Daddy make a big deal about getting us cleaned up before we go to church. That's 'cause they forget that people are like jelly donuts; the best part is on the inside.

Parents forget the best part of a toy is on the inside too. All the fun stays locked inside a toy until someone plays with it and lets the fun out. That's why when my friend Sarah plays with a toy, I want it too. But Mommy doesn't remember. She says, "Lori, you just want that toy because Sarah is playing with it." Well, duh!

Some parents even forget to play with their kids. Can you believe that? They forget 'cause they get busy. They get busy 'cause that's what makes them feel important. I feel important when they stop being busy and play with me, like Daddy did yesterday. You should have seen us, Tommy. Daddy played tag with Sarah and me. When we finished playing, Daddy told Mommy, "It has been years since I played tag. I forgot how much fun it is." See what I mean about forgetting?

Some parents don't play with their kids. That makes no sense. Why do parents have children and not play with them? Playing is one of the funnest things in the whole wide world.

Anyway, Grandma finished the dishes and went into the basement, and Grandpa hasn't checked on me yet, so now I can tell you the really bad news and my secret plan to keep us from moving. Are you listening, Tommy? Last week I told you the real estate lady was going to talk to Mommy and Daddy about selling our house. She came, and you forgot to scream and cry! I even took your pacifier, and you still didn't cry. Thanks a lot, Tommy!

Mommy and Daddy talked to the lady, and they decided they want to sell the house and move. And now there's a big, ugly sign in our yard telling people our house is for sale. I told Daddy, "I don't want the sign right there 'cause it's right where Teddy Bear and I pretend we're camping."

So Daddy moved it over. Then I said, "No! Now the sign is right where we play circus." Our dog, Rascal, is the lion, I'm the lion tamer, and Teddy Bear does tricks. Daddy said, "I'd like to see your circus." I told him, "I don't feel like playing circus 'cause I don't want us to move."

Daddy said, "They offered me a very good job. We'll move to Detroit, we'll buy a nice house, and we'll bring our backyard swing with us." He hugged me and said, "I love you." Then he went in the kitchen to use the phone.

I ran to my room, lay on my bed, and cried. I told Teddy Bear what Daddy said, and Teddy didn't know what to say.

Everything will be ruined if we move. I don't want to move to a dumb old town, live in a dumb old house, and live next door to dumb old kids who play dumb old games. Sheesh!

So here's our secret plan, Tommy. When somebody comes to look at our house 'cause they might want to buy it, you have to cry, scream, and kick. When Mommy gives you the pacifier, spit it out.

Don't forget this time. Forgetting is for grown-ups. I hope this works, 'cause if it doesn't, I don't know what I'm going to do.

TAKE-AWAY VALUE

Think About It

The impending move upsets Lori because she is not good at envisioning the future. That means it's hard for her to imagine how life in the new town could be enjoyable.

Your child is probably the same way. Remember this when he or she gets upset when it's time to leave a friend's house, get out of the pool, or put away the toys. Your youngster is keenly aware how much fun he or she is having right now. But the notion that the future could also be pleasant is pretty vague.

What can you do? First, understand your preschooler's perspective. This will help you stay more patient. Second, when a meltdown begins, recognize it as a distress signal that says, "Help! I'm stuck in my feelings!" Then direct the child's attention to a different set of thoughts and feelings. Do this by racing him or her to the car when it's time to go. Or you can say, "It's time to put away the toys. I bet you can't guess what we're having for a snack tonight."

Talk About It

1. Describe a time when you felt a letdown because a really good time was ending.
2. What strategies did you use to cope?
3. When does your child get upset because the fun is ending?
4. How can you help your child by redirecting his or her attention?

Try It

Make a plan for dealing with your child's emotions when the fun ends.

Chapter 5

Grown-ups Say the Darndest Things

Tuesday, March 30th

GREETINGS AND SALIVATIONS, Tommy. That's how grown-ups say "Hello." That's 'cause they talk funny. They talk way different than kids. And 'cause they talk different, sometimes they don't understand how we talk. But I figgered it out, and I'll explain it to you. But first, there's more bad news. Real bad.

This morning, some people looked at our house 'cause they might want to buy it. You remembered our secret plan, didn't you? You cried, screamed, and kicked your legs, and when Mommy gave you the pacifier, you spit it out. That was great, Tommy! Now Mommy knows you don't want to move either.

When they were walking out of our house, I heard those people say, "If we buy this house, we should cut down the tree in the front yard." They can't cut down my favorite tree! Sheesh!

When they were done looking at the house, I asked Mommy, "Are they going to buy our house?" She said, "The realtor will let us know." This is bad, Tommy. Really bad.

Anyway, like I said before, grown-ups talk funny. They use big words to talk about stuff. Yesterday, when Daddy gave Mommy some flowers, she said, "Oh, what a lovely bouquet." I told her, "It's not a bouquet. It's flowers." She said, "*Bouquet* is a word for a bunch of flowers." Grown-ups even have fancy words for people, Tommy. So they talk about two kinds of people—women and men. But I figgered it out. A girl is a female, and a boy is an e-mail.

And here's what really bugs me. Grown-ups don't just talk funny. They listen funny, too. They're so used to the way they talk they can't understand the way *we* talk. Kids use "kidtalk," which is how we talk about our feelings. Like when a family visits a friend's house, after a while, the mommy says, "It's time to go home." Then the child says, "No! I barely got to play!" But grown-ups don't understand kidtalk, so they think it's a complaint. But that was the child's way of saying, "Thank you for bringing me. I had a wonderful time."

Then on the way home, the kid will ask, "Why did we have to leave?" The parents will say, "Because it's late, and we need to get a good night's sleep." But the kid will keep asking why they had to leave, and after a couple of minutes, the parents get mad. They say, "Stop asking why we have to go. I've told you ten times!"

We keep asking "why?" 'cause we're upset about leaving, and it's our way of asking our parents to help us feel better. It sounds to grown-ups like we want reasons, but we don't. We want help with our feelings. But they keep giving reasons, so we keep asking 'cause they haven't helped us with our feelings.

Grown-ups forget that us kids think with our feelings, 'cause with grown-ups, everything is reasons. So when I'm naughty, Mommy looks for a reason. She asks me, "Why did you take my special necklace without asking?" There wasn't a reason, Tommy. I just really wanted to do it. Grown-ups shouldn't ask us why we're naughty. Lots of times we don't know why. All of a sudden, we really want to do something bad, so we do it. Instead of asking us why we did it, grown-ups should just tell us it was wrong and give us a timeout. Sheesh!

Last night, I think Mommy remembered kidtalk. Our whole family went to Sarah's house and played tag and stuff. Do you remember? It was the funnest night ever. Then Mommy said, "It's time to go home." When I asked her why, she said, "I'm sad, and I don't want to go home either. I was having a really fun time, too!" Then I stopped asking her why we had to go. I knew she was upset too, and that helped me with my feelings.

Us kids are all about what we feel. But parents don't know this, so they give us reasons instead of saying something to help us feel better. It's like we're drowning in our feelings and instead of throwing us a life jacket, they holler at us to swim to shore.

This is real important, Tommy. You have to get this. Listen to what happened yesterday. I played tag with Mommy and Daddy in the backyard. You were in the stroller. Then Mommy said, "It's time to stop playing and get ready for bed." I said, "No! Why do I have to go to bed?" Mommy said, "Playing tag with you and Daddy was the most fun I had all day." And Daddy said, "Lori, you are a fast runner, but I bet I can beat you to the house." Mommy hollered, "Go!" and Daddy ran pretty fast, but I still beat him to the back door.

And then I wasn't so upset, 'cause they helped me with my feelings. Mommy helped me by saying I am fun to play with. Daddy helped me by racing me to the house.

I think they're learning that when I ask, "Why?" it may sound like I want reasons, but I don't. I want help with my feelings. I wish more grown-ups would stop listening to what we're saying, so they could hear what we're feeling.

TAKE-AWAY VALUE

Think About It

Chapter five focuses on discovering your child's feelings. To understand your preschooler's feelings, imagine a sailboat without a crew. The boat goes where the wind pushes it. Preschoolers are like that because their feelings drive them, like the wind directs sailboats.

Since our children's feelings are so important, helping them with their emotions becomes a key task of parenting and grandparenting. Here's a powerful strategy— eagerly look for chances to compliment them on things they do well. Say, "You did a good job getting dressed!" Tell them, "I really like your smile." Say, "I love it when you say 'please.'" Statements like these encourage positive behavior in your child by establishing a positive emotion.

Discipline remains important, but a child who receives regular praise will not need to be disciplined as often. That's because a child's behavior improves when his or her mood brightens. We do that by pointing out what they do well.

Talk About It

1. Tell a story from your childhood when you experienced strong emotions.
2. How did adults respond? How did their response make you feel?
3. How would you feel if someone praised you for the good things you do?
4. How will your youngster feel if you praise the positive things they do?

Try It

Compliment the positive things your child or grandchild does.

Chapter 6

Does Grandpa Know Why?

Tuesday, April 6th

TOMMY, ARE YOU awake? I heard Mommy say you're almost three months old. Now that you're a little older, I can tell you some stuff that's harder to understand.

When you learn to talk, remember to ask lots of questions. On Saturday, after Daddy played basketball in the driveway with his friends, I asked him, “Why did you put both hands up?” He said, “I was letting the other guy know I was open, so he could pass me the ball.”

Today I asked Mommy some questions. I asked her, “Why do you call me so many names?” She calls me “Lori,” “Lorikins,” and “Princess Loreli.” I asked her, “How come you don’t just call me ‘Lori’?” She said, “Just one name can’t hold all the love I feel for you. That’s why we have lots of names for God. We call him ‘Shepherd,’ ‘Savior,’ and ‘Redeemer.’” And there were some other big words I can’t remember. She said, “Just one name can’t hold all the love we feel for him.”

Sometimes I ask our dog, Rascal, some questions. Today I asked her, “Do you know that Mommy and Daddy are trying to sell our house?” She barked, so that means, “Yes.” I asked her, “Do you want to move?” She barked, so that means, “No.” Then I told Rascal, “I need your help ’cause Mommy and Daddy are stubborn about moving. So will you bark when somebody visits our house to see if they want to buy it?” She barked, so that means, “Yes.” I’m glad Rascal will help us. See how good it is to ask questions, Tommy?

On Sunday, I asked Mommy some questions about church. We had a different preacher at our church. During the singing part, he lifted his arms in the air. Our preacher doesn’t do that, so I asked Mommy, “Why did he put his arms up?" She told me, "That's the way he likes to worship God." I guess Mommy's right, but I figgered out another reason. I told her, "He raises his hands to let God know he's open."

I ask Grandpa questions, too. Last Tuesday, when I got ready for bed, I asked him, "Why does it get dark at night?" He said, "God pulls a blanket over the sky to tuck the whole world in bed." So I asked, "How come we see stars if there's a blanket over the earth?" He said, "God pokes holes in the blanket to let in a little light, like a nightlight." I asked Grandpa, "If the moon is big, and the holes are little, how come we can see the moon?" He said, "God made one big hole for the moon." I asked him, "Can a star hole get bigger and turn into a moon?" Grandpa said, "No." I asked him, "Why not?" He said, "God won't let the star holes get bigger." I think Grandpa was trying to pull the wool over my ears.

Then I asked, "Why did God give the stars and the moon for nightlights when we have our own nightlight inside?" He said, "It's so the animals won't be afraid to go to sleep." I asked him, "If God makes it dark and tucks the whole world in bed, how come kids go to bed way before grown-ups?" Then Grandpa smiled and asked me, "How come you ask so many questions?"

Then he asked me, "What could a grandpa do if he had a granddaughter that he loved a lot?" I said, "He could tell her he loves her." So he looked me in the eye and said, "I love you, Lori." He asked, "What could the grandpa do if he told her, but there was still more love in his heart?" I said, "The grandpa could tell her a story."

Then he asked me, "What kind of story should it be?" So I told him, "It should be about a girl who used to be little, but now she's big 'cause now she's four years old. She is hardly ever naughty, and she has a baby brother." (You didn't think I'd forget you, did you, Tommy?) So Grandpa told me a story about a big girl who took her baby brother in the stroller, and they went into a magical forest.

When Grandpa finished the story, he asked, "What could the grandpa do if he told a story, and there was still more love for his granddaughter left over in his heart?" I told him, "The grandpa could make up a song and sing it for her." He said, "I'm not very good at making up songs real fast." So he sang me a song somebody else wrote. It's about a singing frog. When he sang it, I laughed and laughed. When he finished, I said, "Sing it again!" So he did.

Then Grandpa asked me, "What could a grandpa do if he said 'I love you,' told a story, and sang a song, but there was still more love for his granddaughter in his heart?" I said, "He could give her a hug." And you know what Tommy? That's what Grandpa did.

TAKE-AWAY VALUE

Think About It

In this chapter, Lori asked lots of questions. When you face many questions, determine if they are complaining questions or curiosity questions. Complaining questions center on things like, "Why do I have to go to bed?" and "Why can't I have another cookie?" Curiosity questions center on things like, "How come birds fly?" and "Why is the sky blue?"

Children ask complaining questions over and over. They keep asking them because they are upset. As an adult, you understand that scratching a mosquito bite does not provide lasting relief. In a similar fashion, repetitively asking a complaining question does not help the child feel better.

The child who repeatedly asks, "Why do I have to go to bed now?" doesn't need another explanation. That child is stuck in a rut and needs help getting out. As mentioned in the Take-away section following chapter four, try distracting your youngster with an alternate activity.

But some questions are curiosity questions. Examples include, "Why do cats meow?" and "How come we only see the stars at night?" When responding to these questions, remember two things. First, recognize it's a teachable moment because the child is interested. Take advantage of this by answering the question and briefly adding something else. When your preschooler asks, "Why is the sky blue?" say, "When the sunlight comes through the air, it turns blue. Wasn't God smart to figure out how to do that?" Second, enjoy the fact that these questions are one way your child expresses a desire to communicate with you.

Talk About It

1. As an adult, what was a question you really wanted an answer to?
2. How did you feel toward the person who gave you a good answer? Or how did you feel toward the person who could have answered, but didn't?
3. What questions does your child ask you?
4. What do you enjoy about the questions, and what bothers you about them?

Try It

The next time you get complaining questions, recognize that your child is emotionally stuck and needs your help.

Chapter 7

Oh No!

Tuesday, April 13th

TOMMY, SOMETHING TERRIBLE happened! Rascal's gone! It just happened. Grandpa and Grandma came over to babysit us, like they always do on Tuesday, and Mommy and Daddy went out to eat. Just before Mommy and Daddy left, they put Rascal in the backyard to play. They didn't chain her up 'cause we have a fence around the backyard.

After Mommy and Daddy left, Grandma and I sat on the living room couch while we read some books she got from the library. Then I played hide-and-seek with Grandpa in the basement. When we finished playing, Grandpa said, "Lori, it's raining. Put your coat on, and bring Rascal in from the backyard." I went outside and looked for Rascal, and she wasn't there!

I ran into the house and yelled, "Grandpa! Grandma! Rascal's gone! Rascal's gone!" I had to say it a couple of times 'cause I was crying so hard that they couldn't understand me. Grandpa grabbed an umbrella and looked all around in the backyard, but Rascal wasn't there. Grandma looked through every room in the house. She called, "Rascal, Rascal," and looked under beds and in closets. Grandma told me, "Check in the garage." I did, but she wasn't there, either.

What are we going to do? You don't know how much I love Rascal. You're just a baby, and you've only known Rascal a few months, but she's the only dog I've ever had. And now I'll probably never see her again.

Since we didn't find Rascal, Grandma called Mommy and Daddy and told them what happened. When they got home, Daddy said, "Tell me everything that happened with Rascal tonight." So I did. Then he asked, "Do you know anything else about where Rascal might be?" I told him, "Rascal promised to bark and growl so we wouldn't have to move, and now maybe she ran away so she wouldn't have to leave St. Louis." Daddy said, "Thank you for telling me that, but that's not the reason Rascal is gone." Then he looked me in the eye and said, "I will do everything I can to get our dog back."

Then Daddy went into the backyard and spent a long time looking around. When he came back in, he said, "There's a spot that has been dug out under the fence, and that's probably how she got out."

Grandma said, "I'm so sorry this happened." She hugged me and asked, "Would you like a cookie?" I said, "No," 'cause I was too sad about Rascal being gone.

Daddy went over to Sarah's house next door and asked for help looking for Rascal. So Daddy and I went to some houses, Mommy went to some, and Sarah's Daddy went to some houses. Grandma and Grandpa stayed at the house to be with you and to answer the phone in case somebody called to say they found Rascal.

One of the houses Daddy and I went to is where Jimmy Brodnick lives. One time Jimmy told me, "I'm better than you 'cause I'm five, and you're only four, Lori. And girls are dumb."

I told Daddy, "I don't want to go to Jimmy's house 'cause he's mean. He calls me names, and one time he had a whole bag of candy bars. Jimmy asked, 'Do you want one?' and held it out to me. When I reached for it, he pulled it back, opened the wrapper, ate the whole thing, and said, 'Ha, ha' to me." Daddy said, "That was mean, but Jimmy won't do anything bad this time when I'm standing beside you."

Daddy knocked on the door and talked to Jimmy's mommy. He asked, "Have you seen our dog?" She said, "No." Jimmy stood next to his mother. Then he went to a window, stuck his tongue out at me, and shook his fist at me. Daddy didn't see it 'cause he was talking to Mrs. Brodnick. I hate that Jimmy Brodnick.

Daddy and I went home after going to some more houses. Nobody knew where Rascal was. When we got home, Daddy called the animal shelter, but Rascal wasn't there either. He called some of his friends and told them Rascal is A.W.O.L. I figgered out that A.W.O.L stands for "America Online."

Do you know where she went, Tommy? If you can find her, I'll never take your pacifier again. I promise.

Everything bad happens to me. First Mommy and Daddy said we're going to move, and now Rascal ran away. Tommy, you're still too young to understand what love is like. But let me tell you, 'cause I know. When you love somebody, it's the funnest thing in the whole wide world. You feel happy inside and want to jump around and stuff. And then when they're gone, it's like your tummy is a bright red birthday balloon that got popped.

Oh, Tommy...what are we going to do?

TAKE-AWAY VALUE

Think About It

Lori feels devastated because her dog ran away. How should you respond when your child experiences a loss?

First, listen to your child. Look your child in the eye as he or she talks. Don't interrupt. Offer a hug. This type of listening communicates powerfully that you care. Second, talk to your child about what happened. If it impacts you, express your sorrow. If it doesn't, share how sad you are because of your child's loss. Third, do something. If you can fix the problem, do it. But if you can't, do something to address the child's feelings. Lori's parents looked for the dog.

What could you do? Here are some examples. When a grandparent dies, give the child something that belonged to the grandparent, such as a keepsake or some jewelry. If your child's best friend moves away, take pictures of the two kids as a tangible reminder of the friend. Or arrange for a special, fun time for the two kids before moving day.

Talk About It

1. Describe a difficult experience you had as an adult or as a child.
2. How did people respond to your need during this time? Did they help you feel better?
3. What difficult experiences has your child had?
4. How did you help your child through that experience?

Try It

Choose something to do the next time your child experiences a loss.

Chapter 8

Guess What I Saw

Tuesday, April 20th

DID YOU HEAR me yell last night, Tommy? Did you wonder what was happening? There were monsters in my closet! Great big, hairy, scary, real ones! So I hugged Teddy Bear real tight, scrunched my eyes shut, and screamed, "MOMM-EEE!"

When she came in my room, I told her, "There's monsters in my closet!" She sat on my bed, put her hand on my shoulder, and asked, "Are you upset about Rascal being gone?" I said, "I miss Rascal and still cry about that, but I'm scared about the monsters. They're real. I saw them." She said, "Do you know that you can ask Jesus to help you when you're scared?" I told her, "Yes, but they were so scary, it was hard to think about praying." Mommy hugged me. She whispered in my ear, "I love you. I'll be right back. I'm going to get something to get rid of the monsters."

Then she left my room and came back with a can. It was hard to tell, with only my night-light on, but it looked like air freshener. But she said, "This is monster spray." She walked right up to the open closet and sprayed. I screamed at her, "Don't stand so close to the closet 'cause the monsters might grab you with their claw thingys!" While she was spraying, my arms and legs were shaking, and I pulled the blanket over my head.

Mommy sprayed a little more and told me, "The monsters are gone now." The room smelled real good. Mommy didn't say why, but I figgered it out. Those monsters were stinky, and when they left, the room smelled better.

I told her, "Spray under the bed and behind the door, too. And you should stay in the room in case they come back." She told me, "The spray won't let them come back." I said, "Leave a can of monster spray with me in case some other monsters come." She said, "The spray will keep the other monsters out, too." I told her, "I'm still scared of monsters."

She said, "They won't come back." I asked her, "But what if they do?" She said, "Daddy will grab them, stuff them in a high chair, put a baby's bib on them, and tickle their feet till they scream for their mommies." I giggled, and Teddy Bear thought it was funny, too. Laughing helped me not be scared.

I told Mommy, "I wish Rascal was here to protect me." Mommy said, "You miss her, don't you?" I said, "Uh huh, 'cause Rascal would know what to do." You see, Tommy, monsters are scared of dogs. But since Rascal isn't here, I'm still a little scared of monsters.

And then I got a great idea, Tommy. I asked Mommy, "Do we always have to tell the truth?" She said, "Yes." So I told her, "We have to tell the real estate lady the truth that our house has monsters, so she can tell people not to buy our house." Mommy smiled, hugged me, and said, "I love my persistent daughter."

Sometimes I'm not scared of monsters or anything, but I can't go to sleep if I'm not sleepy. One night, when Grandpa and Grandma were babysitting us at our house, Grandpa said, "It's time for you to go to bed, and I'll tuck you in." I told him, "I'm not tired." He shook his head a little and said, "That's too bad. I made up a bedtime story for you." I asked him, "Is it a plain old story, or is it extra special?" He said, "It's extra special." Then I asked him, "Is it super-duper extra special or just extra special?" He said, "I'm not sure if it's super-duper, but it's about a girl who used to be little but isn't little anymore now that she is four years old." I told Grandpa, "I'm not tired, but Teddy Bear is a little sleepy, so you can tell the story to help Teddy fall asleep."

So he told me the story, and it was as good as the books that Grandma brings from the library. The story was about Princess Loreli, who went to a kingdom where she became a princess. Then the witch stole all the kids' bedtime storybooks. After that, none of the children could fall asleep at bedtime. Every night, they cried 'cause their parents had no books to read to them. So the parents brought their children to Princess Loreli. Every night, she made up a story for the children, and they fell asleep as soon as the story ended.

But Princess Loreli wanted the books back, Tommy. She walked into the forest, found the witch's cottage, grabbed the books, and ran back to the castle. The witch realized how smart and strong Princess Loreli was, and the witch never bothered the kids again. So the children got their books back, and they fell asleep every night after their parents read to them.

Grandpa's story ended there. He said, "Good night," prayed with me, hugged me, and left the room. I hollered, "Come back, Grandpa! Your hug's already wearing off." So he came back, and this time when he hugged me, he said, "I'm hugging you through the blanket. It's called a 'blanket hug.' A blanket hug soaks into the blanket, kind of like butter and syrup soak into a pancake. You can't see the butter and syrup, but they're there. A blanket hug is the same way. And a blanket hug stays in the blanket all night long."

I thought Grandpa was going to leave my room, but he wasn't done. He gave me another blanket hug and said, "I love you bigger than the sky." So I said, "I love you bigger than the stars." He said, "I wouldn't trade you for all the money in the whole world." That made me smile. So I said, "I wouldn't trade you for all the candy in the whole world. And you aren't just a special Grandpa. You are a super-duper, extra special Grandpa." And that made Grandpa smile.

TAKE-AWAY VALUE

Think About It

Because adults think logically, we often try to prove a child's fear is unrealistic. But giving logical information to a kid who's afraid of monsters or spiders rarely douses the flames of fear.

A better response is to do something. Lori's mother responded creatively, but more ordinary actions help too. Give a hug, move a nightlight, bring a drink, or divert the child's attention away from what's scaring him or her. Communicate with words and body language that you care about the youngster's feelings. Kids know that monsters, spiders, or boogey men under the bed are no match for a sympathetic parent.

Talk About It

1. What frightened you as a child?
2. How did your parents respond to your fears?
3. What is your child afraid of?
4. What action could you take to show you care and to alleviate your child's fear?

Try It

If your child experiences a recurring fear, decide on a few things you could do the next time he or she is afraid.

Chapter 9

Look What I Found

Tuesday, April 27th

GUESS WHAT HAPPENED, Tommy. Mommy took us for a walk, and you fell asleep in the stroller, so you missed it. I was walking slow 'cause I was still so sad and missing Rascal.

All of a sudden I ran away from Mommy. She yelled, "Come back, Lori!" But I kept running. I had to 'cause I saw Rascal at the end of the block. She was skinny and had dirt all over her. I hollered, "Rascal! Rascal!" and ran toward her with my arms out. She barked and ran to me. When I bent over to hug her, she jumped up, knocked me over, and got my shirt dirty. But I didn't care 'cause I was so happy, and when Rascal licked the tears off my cheeks, it tickled. I laughed and hugged her tight.

I hollered, "Mommy! It's Rascal!" Mommy was already running and pushing the stroller as fast as she could. When she got there, she cried and hugged Rascal and me at the same time.

She took out her cell phone, called Daddy, and told him I found Rascal. It was hard for her to hear Daddy 'cause Rascal barked so much. She got off the phone and told me, "Daddy's really happy, and he promised to pick up some Imo's pizza for supper to celebrate." I told Mommy, "If we're going to celebrate, we should have cookies, too." She said, "That's a good idea."

Then we walked back to our house. While Mommy gave Rascal a bath, she said, "Lori, Rascal's doggie collar is gone. Do you know where it is?" I told her, "Since you wouldn't let me play with your special necklace, I thought maybe I could play with Rascal's a little bit." Mommy said,

"Leave the collar on all the time. That collar had our address and phone number on it."

I asked Mommy, "How did Rascal get food when she was gone?" Mommy said, "I don't know. Maybe she got food from a doggie dish somebody left outside or by tipping over a garbage can." I asked Mommy, "Why didn't Rascal come back sooner?" Mommy said, "She was probably lost and didn't know how to find us."

Mommy dried Rascal off and gave her some food and water. Then Mommy took me into the living room. She said, "There's a story in the Bible kind of like Rascal coming home. A young man went far away from home where he spent all his money, because he bought whatever he wanted. Then he realized he needed to go back home. His daddy saw him coming, ran to him, and hugged him even though the son was all dirty. The daddy was so happy to have him home that he threw a big party." I asked Mommy, "Did they have pizza and cookies?" She said, "No, but they had some other really good food."

Mommy said, "That story is really about how much God loves us. He wants us to come back to him just like that daddy wanted his son to come home and just like we wanted Rascal to come home. If we tell God we're sorry for the bad things we've done, believe that Jesus died for our sin, and ask him to take control of our lives, he'll save us."

I told Mommy, "I didn't know that God loved me so much, and I want to ask Jesus to forgive me. I promise I'll never run away from home, and I'll never dig a hole under the fence."

So she read me some Bible verses. Rascal was done eating and sat on my lap. I petted her, and Mommy helped me pray. I smooshed my eyes shut real tight, so I wouldn't peek, and I prayed like this:

> "Dear Mister God, I'm sorry for the bad stuff I've done. I'm sorry for disobeying Mommy and Daddy sometimes. I'm sorry for taking Mommy's special necklace and Rascal's collar without asking, and for hiding Tommy's pacifier one time when he was crying a lot and getting on my nerves. And I'm sorry for what I did to Jimmy Brodnick at the neighborhood picnic. He was mean and called me names. So when he took off his shoes to jump on the trampoline, I went to the food table, got some whip cream, and put it in the toes of Jimmy's shoes. I'm sorry for doing that.
>
> I'm glad Jesus died for my sin. Please take it all away. And help me to be good 'cause sometimes it's real hard. Amen."

Right after I prayed, Mommy hugged me. She said, "I'm so happy! Lorikins, you're never too little and your sins are never too big for God to forgive." Mommy's right. I'm not too little. I'm four and a half, and that's almost the same as being five years old.

Then Mommy took out her cell phone again. She called Daddy, and she had tears in her eyes. She told him, "I have the best news! Lori just prayed and asked Jesus into her heart!"

After all that, I was pretty thirsty, so Mommy poured me some juice. Just before I drank it, I hollered, "Look out Jesus!" Mommy asked, "Why did you say that?" I said, "You told Daddy that Jesus is in my heart. I had to warn Jesus so he could move over and not get wet when I drank my juice."

Tommy, you've got to listen to me. Being a Christian is the best thing that ever happened to me in my whole entire life. You should be a Christian too! And if all this stuff is hard to understand, don't worry. I'll figger it out and explain it to you. That's what a big sister is for.

TAKE-AWAY VALUE

Think About It

Can most preschoolers understand as much about God as Lori did in this chapter? Most can't, but some can. You can nurture your youngster's understanding of God if you provide both structured and unstructured learning opportunities.

Structured opportunities are planned and regular. Examples include Sunday school, family devotions after supper, or Bible stories read at bedtime. Unstructured learning opportunities come spontaneously and vary from day to day. Lori's mother took advantage of an unstructured opportunity by pointing out the similarity between finding Rascal and the parable of the prodigal son. You can use unstructured opportunities, too. Point out the beauty of nature, and ask, "Why did God make flowers so pretty?" Pray with your child about finding a lost toy. When a friend is sick, ask, "What does Jesus want us to do to encourage that person?"

Talk About It

1. What is something that you have come to enjoy because someone talked about it with you? Examples could include things such as a hobby, restaurant, vacation spot, or book.
2. Does talking with your child about God feel comfortable or awkward? Why?
3. What helps you talk to your child about God? What hinders you?
4. What can you do about the things that make it hard to talk about God?

Try it

Choose one suggestion from your discussion, and use it with your child.

Chapter 10

Heigh-ho, Heigh-ho

Tuesday, May 4th

YOU MISSED IT, Tommy. Mommy took you to Grandma and Grandpa's house. And she took me to Daddy's work for "Take your daughter to work" day. I was so excited 'cause when Mommy and Daddy do stuff with me, it makes me feel special.

And I liked going 'cause it got me away from hearing what Jimmy Brodnick says when I play outside. He says, "Ha, ha. We're going to Florida to see Mickey Mouse at the Magic Kingdom® and the Apricot Center. You probably won't even get a vacation." But today I went to Daddy's work, and I didn't have to listen to Jimmy.

Our Daddy is smart, and he helps people fix problems with computers. He is a consultant. That means he doesn't really have a job, he just tells other people how to do their jobs. When Daddy tells people he works for a company called "Cybertooth Tiger," they laugh. But I don't know why. Tigers aren't funny. They're scary.

Work is real important to grown-ups. That's why they have jobs, and why they ask us kids what kind of work we want to do when we grow up. And when they aren't working, they like to pretend they are working. So Daddy plays in the garage and calls it "working on the car." Mommy plays in the dirt and calls it "working in the garden." And Daddy puts on play clothes and exercises and calls it "working out." You see, Tommy, if you want adults to do something, you have to make it sound like work, even if it's really play.

But kids aren't like that. If you want us to work, you have to make it seem like play. I think Mommy knows this. When she says, "It's time to pick up the toys," I say, "No!" and keep playing 'cause putting away toys is work. But then she makes it seem like play. She says, "I bet I can put those toys away faster than you, Princess Loreli." That makes it a game, so I put the toys away super fast, and she says, "Hey! You beat me!" Then she says, "I bet I can beat you up the stairs." But I'm fast, and I always beat her.

She always tells me, "When you have work that must be done, find a way to make it fun." It's nice having a smart Mommy.

Anyway, when Mommy was driving me to Daddy's office, she was singing, "Heigh-ho, heigh-ho, it's off to work we go." And then she whistled a little bit. When we got to Daddy's work, she took me to his office. I helped him a lot. We made copies and cleaned his office. He needed new pictures for the walls, so I drew some, and we put them up.

Lots of Daddy's friends talked to me. They asked me, "What do you want to do when you grow up?" I said, "I want to be a teacher, like my Grandpa."

And when it was time to go, one of the ladies said, "Thank you for coming in. You are a pretty smart girl." I told her, "I didn't used to be this smart back when I was little, but now that I'm four and a half years old, it's easy to be smart."

Then Daddy's boss asked me, "Did you have a good time?" I told him, "It was kind of fun, but I never got to meet any of those clowns Daddy says he works with." Daddy's boss smiled real big and said, "That's very interesting." He bent down and asked, "Did your father mention any of the clowns' names?" Right away, Daddy scooped me up in his arms, and said, "We have to hurry or we'll be late meeting Mommy for lunch."

We drove home to pick up Mommy, and then we went out to eat. Daddy told Mommy, "Lori was a big girl and helped a lot." When we got to the restaurant, Daddy paid a man to park the car for him. It's called "ballet parking." The restaurant was pretty fancy. They had soft napkins, slurp du jour, and everything.

When we ate our food, I asked Mommy and Daddy, "Are we going to have a vacation? Jimmy keeps bugging me about his vacation." Mommy said, "Daddy and I need to talk that over. I'm not sure I'm ready to take a vacation with a baby yet."

The worst stuff always happens to me! First, our parents told us we're going to move. Then Rascal ran away, and now we probably won't even get a vacation.

I felt crabby until we finished eating and Mommy took a small package out of her coat pocket. It was long, skinny, and wrapped in shiny silver paper. She handed it to me and said, "This is for you. You may open it." When I opened it, I found a pretty necklace. Mommy reminded me to say "thank you" and helped me put it on. She said, "Now that you're getting bigger, you may have your own necklace, and now you won't need to take my special necklace without asking." I *love* my necklace, Tommy!

So it's pretty easy being a grown-up. All you have to do is go to work, play with some fun machines for a couple of hours, and then you get to eat out at a fancy restaurant.

Going to Daddy's work made me tired. Now I really need a vacation. I hope we're going to have one.

TAKE-AWAY VALUE

Think About It

This chapter illustrates motivating kids to do chores by turning the behavior into a game. Because play fascinates children, you can often motivate them to obey if you turn your request into a game.

Do this by tapping into your child's vivid imagination. Your child could be a weightless astronaut floating in the bedroom while making a bed, a big truck hauling dirty dishes to the sink (complete with truck noises), or a princess putting away the royal toys so the dragon can't get them. Set a timer and pretend it's for a bomb. See if your child can finish the chore before the timer beeps and the bomb explodes.

If you have a playful spirit and an active imagination, this approach may come easily to you. If not, this strategy will require effort on your part. But it will be worth it, because you'll have a more cooperative child.

Talk About It

1. What strategies do you use to motivate yourself to do unpleasant tasks?
2. What things does your child resist doing when you tell him or her to do it?
3. Explain why some chores are difficult for your child.
4. Share examples of how you have turned a chore into a game.

Try It

Choose a behavior that your kids resist doing, and turn it into a game.

Chapter 11

Yippee!

Tuesday, May 11th

TOMMY! TOMMY! MOMMY and Daddy just told me the best news in the whole wide world! Oh...Oh...I have to catch my breath...We're *not* going to move! That means my plan worked! I just knew that if you and me and Rascal all tried our hardest, Mommy and Daddy would change their minds.

Mommy and Daddy told me during supper, just before Grandma and Grandpa came over. You were sleeping then, but you're awake now so I'll tell you all about it. We're not moving 'cause the man who wanted to hire Daddy got fired. So he can't give Daddy a job. And we're staying here in St. Louis in this house, near Grandma and Grandpa, and next door to my best friend, Sarah.

The best stuff always happens to me. Rascal came back, I got to see Daddy's work, and now we're not going to move! Yippee!

Mommy and Daddy still haven't decided if we're going to take a vacation. But Mommy said, "Daddy and I will talk about it, and we'll tell you our decision next week." I hope we do take a vacation 'cause Jimmy keeps bragging about his.

Anyway, when I found out during supper that we're not moving, I jumped out of my chair, and hollered, "We're not moving! We're not moving!" And I ran all over the house. Daddy told me, "Come back, and sit down at the table." I did, but I could barely stay in my chair.

Daddy smiled and said, "You have the worst case of wiggles I've ever seen. The only cure is a wiggle contest. And if you sit still for seven more minutes and eat some more supper, you may choose who goes first in the wiggle contest." That meant I had to sit real still and eat more, 'cause in a wiggle contest, you have to make the other person go first, so you know how to wiggle better than him.

Daddy set a timer for seven minutes. It was hard, but I stayed in my chair and ate my food. When the timer rang, Mommy said, "Daddy, I think Lori sat very well and ate a lot of supper, so she gets to choose who goes first."

So I told Daddy, "You go first." He wiggled pretty good. He wiggled his arms, then one leg at a time, and then his head. At the end, he closed one eye and wiggled one arm back and forth over his head. Then I got a little worried 'cause I knew it was going to be real hard to beat him.

I knew I'd have to give my best wiggle, so I asked Mommy to get the CD and turn on *The Nutcracker Sweet* by Chy Kopsky. That's classical music, and Mommy and I dance around the house to it.

When the music started, I wiggled as hard as I could—up and down, and side to side along with the music. Since Daddy had put one arm in the air and closed one eye, I put *both* arms in the air, closed *both* eyes, and only peeked twice.

Mommy and Daddy clapped when I was done, and Mommy said, "You both did a very good job, but I think Lori won." Daddy said, "That was fun." But how could it be fun for Daddy? He lost.

Mommy and Daddy are smart. They know I have to move if I'm going to be good. And they know it's even funner when I get to move and use my imagination at the same time. Last week, Mommy was my Sunday school teacher 'cause our reg'lar teacher was on vacation. When it was time to get a drink, she told us to pretend we were getting into a boat. Then she told us to "row" ourselves down the hall to the drinking fountain. It was so fun to "row" to the water fountain, we forgot all about pushing other kids and being noisy. It's fun being good when I can move around and use my imagination.

That's how our family devotions are. I get to act out the Bible stories after Daddy reads them, and I'm real good at it. Our family devotions used to be dumb. Daddy would read the Bible story and get mad 'cause I couldn't stay in my chair.

But now devotions are fun! Now Daddy reads just a little, and then I get to act out the story. I get to move and use my imagination. I like that.

Yesterday, Daddy read the story about David and Goliath. Then we acted it out. I was David, and Daddy was Goliath. I swung a sock around my head, pretended it was a sling, and threw it at Daddy. After it hit him, he fell down real slow and tried to grab me, give me a hug, and tickle me, but I jumped away.

Then we traded. Daddy was David, and I was Goliath. I stood on a chair so I'd be real tall. Daddy swung a sock around his head and threw it at me, but I ducked 'cause it's no fun being Goliath if you have to be dead.

But sometimes I can't move around, like the last time Mommy cut my hair. She knew it was hard for me to sit still. Since she couldn't let me move around, she let me use my imagination. She said, "Here's a statue pill. It's a pretend pill that helps you sit as still as a statue." She pretended to open a pill bottle and pretended to put a pill in my hand. I pretended to put it in my mouth. She gave me an empty cup, and I pretended to drink the water and swallow the pill.

You know what? That statue pill worked! I sat still. You know, Tommy, to kids, sometimes stuff that's pretend is more real than stuff that is real.

Why won't grown-ups let us be kids? They forget that if they let us move around and use our imaginations, we learn and we're good.

Don't be crabby at grown-ups, Tommy. Just remember what the Bible says about grown-ups. Philippians 1:6 is Grandpa's favorite verse, and it says, "He who began a good work in you still has a long way to go."

TAKE-AWAY VALUE

Think About It

It's hard for young kids when adults think sitting still is the only way to be good. Rather than stifling their urge to move, look for ways to allow movement. At the dinner table, let them be a "special helper" and get up from the table to get something for you that's on the counter. In church, let them be in charge of grabbing the song book when it's needed. In the car, encourage them to help you watch for a landmark. Tell your child, "We need to turn right when we come to the park. Point to it when you see it." In the grocery store, if your child is walking beside you or riding in the cart, let him or her help put food items in the cart.

Talk About It

1. To understand our kids' point of view, how would you feel if you were told to move all the time, and you got scolded every time you stopped moving?
2. In what situations does your child find it difficult to sit still?
3. What could you do to allow some movement in that situation?
4. What strategies have you tried when it's difficult for your child to sit still?

Try It

Make a plan to allow movement in a place where your child has to sit.

Chapter 12

What Makes Mommy Smile

Tuesday, May 18th

WE'RE GOING ON vacation, Tommy! Just before Grandma and Grandpa came over to babysit us tonight, Mommy told me. She smiled big and said, "We're going to a cabin this weekend, and it'll be a lot of fun." It'll just be the six of us. You know, Mommy, Daddy, me, you, Rascal, and Teddy Bear.

And I have to tell you about last weekend, 'cause it was weird, and you probably didn't understand it. On Saturday, Daddy took me to a garage sale. I know about garage sales 'cause Grandpa told me. He said, "Some people call them 'tag sales,' and it's when some people sell stuff they don't want so other people can buy stuff they don't need. You go from house to house and buy things. It's like trick-or-treating for grown-ups." Just before we left for the garage sales, Mommy said, "Don't be gone too long, 'cause I'll miss my sweet girl."

At the garage sales, we bought a travel clock and a coffee mug for Mommy. Daddy said, "The travel clock will be good for our vacation." And I said, "Now that Mommy has another clock, she'll have more time to get stuff done." And she'll use the coffee mug a lot 'cause she loves coffee. When we gave her the mug and the clock, she smiled and said, "Thank you very much."

When I saw how happy she was about the stuff we gave her, I wanted to give her something else. So I went to the front yard and picked dandelions. Jimmy Brodnick walked by and said, "Picking dandelions is dumb." But when I gave them to Mommy, she smiled and said, "I like them a lot." That's 'cause she is way smarter than Jimmy.

Then I thought that if dandelions made Mommy smile, the flowers in our front yard would make her smile too. So I picked some and gave them to her. But they didn't make Mommy smile. She was upset and said, "I know you were trying to be nice, but promise me you'll never take flowers from our yard again." So I promised.

After lunch, I didn't want Mommy to stay mad at me. I remembered my promise about not picking our flowers, so I picked flowers from Sarah's yard next door so Mommy wouldn't be upset. But that didn't make her smile either. She got mad even though I kept my promise. Sheesh! Grown-ups are hard to figure out. Mommy said, "You need to apologize to Sarah's mommy, but first, we should bake brownies for her." I asked her, "Why?" She said, "Sometimes it's good to apologize by saying you're sorry and by giving a gift."

When we made the brownies, Mommy showed me how to test them with a toothpick. You stick a toothpick in the brownies and pull it out. If nothing sticks to the toothpick, the brownies are done.

When they were done, I asked, "Can we cut the brownies in the pan with a pizza cutter?" Mommy asked, "Why?" I said, "The pizza cutter helps pizza taste yummy, so it will make the brownies taste yummy, too." She said, "That's a good idea."

Before we took the brownies next door, Mommy told me what to say. Then we went next door to Sarah's house, and I told Sarah's mommy, "I'm sorry for taking your flowers." She said, "I forgive you. Your apology shows that you're a big girl." I said, "I am a big girl 'cause I'm four and a half years old." Sarah's mommy said, "The brownies look yummy." I said, "They're yummy 'cause we cut them with a pizza cutter and tested them with a toothpick." She smiled and said, "Another way to test them is to eat one." We each ate one, and they were real yummy.

Then we went back to our house. After supper, Mommy took a nap. You napped too. Daddy and I tiptoed into the kitchen, and we made some lemon pudding as a surprise for Mommy. We helped each other a lot. Daddy showed me how to make the pudding, and I showed him how to test the pudding with a toothpick to see if it was ready. Daddy said, "I've never heard of testing pudding with a toothpick." I told him, "Don't feel bad; we all have a lot to learn."

When Mommy woke up, we gave her some. We put the pudding in a bowl, with a cookie on top of the pudding and a spoon stuck in the pudding. Daddy whispered to me, "Mommy will like the treat even more if you say something nice." I didn't know what to say. So Daddy whispered to me to tell Mommy, "Thank you for being a good Mommy." So that's what I told her, and she smiled.

It felt good to make her happy again. She ate some of the pudding and said, "The pudding is wonderful." I told her, "It's yummy 'cause I checked it with a toothpick." She smiled again, hugged me, and said, "Thank you for the pudding and the cookie. I'm lucky to have a sweet girl who wants to give me things. A gift is a great way to cheer someone up."

She was quiet for a while. Then she put her hand on my shoulder, looked at me, and said, "If you want to pick flowers you have to ask me first." I asked, "Does that include our vacation this weekend?" She said, "Yes. You always have to ask first." I asked her, "Does that mean anywhere in the whole wide world?" She said, "Yes."

Then I asked, "Could I pick flowers on the moon without asking you first, like if I'm an astronaut or something?" Mommy smiled and said, "That would be very nice. I've never had moon flowers before." I asked, "What color do you want?" She said, "Either red or yellow ones would be nice." I told her, "Don't worry. I won't stay on the moon for very long. I'll hurry home 'cause I'll miss my sweet Mommy." She smiled bigger than ever and hugged me.

You know, Tommy, a hug is a pretty good gift to give 'cause you don't have to say "sorry" for giving one, and you don't have to use a toothpick to see if it's ready.

TAKE-AWAY VALUE

Think About It

In this chapter, Lori's mother helps Lori learn how to apologize. Her father teaches her the joy of making a surprise for someone else. These incidents illustrate the process of showing our kids how to relate to other people. It's important to teach your child or grandchild valuable relational skills.

Coach your child through it step by step as needed, and give praise generously for a good effort. Teach your youngster how to make friends, share, apologize, make a guest feel welcome, and respond appropriately when someone apologizes to us.

There are two situations that will help you detect that your child needs help with a social skill. First, when your preschooler handles a social interaction badly, it may be because he or she didn't know what to say or do. Second, if your youngster seems very hesitant about an upcoming encounter or conversation, it might be that your child doesn't know how to act in that situation.

Help your child learn a social skill by talking about the situation. Explain why the other people reacted like they did and how your child could handle it differently next time. Give them an example of what they could say next time.

Talk About It

1. Describe a task you couldn't do as an adult until someone showed you how. Examples might include using a computer program or completing a home improvement project.
2. How did you feel when you didn't know how to do it? How did you feel after you learned how to do it?
3. What relational skills does your child need to learn?
4. How could you help your child learn these relational skills?

Try It

Pick a social skill your child needs to learn and explain how to do it.

Chapter 13

When Are We Going to Be There?

Tuesday, May 25th

DID YOU LIKE our vacation, Tommy? I did. I couldn't believe what Mommy and Daddy did, and I haven't had a chance to explain it to you yet.

Here's what they did. The night before our vacation, they talked real quietly in the dining room, like they didn't want me to hear them. That got me interested. I was in the living room playing with Teddy Bear and my red rubber ball. A lot of the red has worn off, but I still play with it. I rolled it into the kitchen to be closer and to hear what Mommy and Daddy were saying. They couldn't see me 'cause I was behind that one part where the kitchen counter sticks out halfway into the room. You should have heard what they said.

Daddy said, "When we take a long trip in the car, I'm tired of the way Lori misbehaves. And I don't like it when she complains over and over, 'When are we going to be there?' So on this trip, let's bring the kitchen timer and set it for fifteen minutes. Every time fifteen minutes goes by and she's been good, she gets a dime. If she acts up, she gets one warning, and if she doesn't stop, she won't get ten cents for that fifteen minutes. We could keep track of how much she earns and give it to her after we get to the cabin."

I tried to breathe real quiet so they wouldn't hear me, but it was hard 'cause I got so excited I wanted to jump up and down. But then Mommy said, "I don't like that idea. We shouldn't have to pay Lori to be good. It sounds like bribing."

Then Daddy said, "Lots of parents give their kids money to spend or buy them a treat on vacation, but this way, she'd have to earn it by being good. Let's try it. If it doesn't work, we won't do it again. But what if it works? How much would it be worth to have a peaceful trip?"

Then Mommy was quiet, and I got scared she wouldn't agree with Daddy. I hugged Teddy Bear real tight and tried not to drop my ball or make any noise. I thought they would hear my heart going *thumpy-thumpy*. Mommy said, "I'm not sure about this, but we could try your idea once."

The next day, when we got in the car to leave for our vacation, Daddy told me about the timer and earning money by being good and not complaining. I think they thought they could trick me, like I was going to be crabby and not earn any dimes, but I tricked them and I earned a whole dollar!

The trip to the cabin was fun. It was fun being good to earn money, and some of the time we played games like counting trucks and "I Spy." And Mommy read me some books that Grandma bought for us.

After we drove a while, Mommy said, "I think we missed our turn. Let's stop and ask for directions." But Daddy said, "I don't think we missed our turn. Let's drive a little longer." So Mommy asked, "Do you know why the three wise men in the Bible are called 'wise?'" Daddy said, "No." She said, "They're called wise because when they couldn't find baby Jesus, they stopped to ask for directions." She laughed and laughed, and Daddy smiled.

We finally got there. It was Bennett Spring State Park. The first night, Daddy made a fire, and we roasted marshmallows. Mommy put one on a stick for me, and I shoved it right into the fire. When it was burning, I pulled it out, and Mommy hollered, "Blow it out, Lori!" So I did. Since it was all black, I said, "I don't want to eat it. You can have it, Daddy." Then I did the whole thing again and again.

The next day, Mommy said, "People like camping because they can get away from it all." I thought that meant leaving lots of stuff behind. But I saw people with big campers that had lots of stuff in them. We met a nice family who had a microwave, refrigerator, toilet, shower, television, and a DVD player in their camper. That's when I figgered it out. To grown-ups, "getting away from it all" means bringing as much of it as you can.

When our vacation was over, we had to drive back home. Mommy and Daddy gave me another chance to earn dimes on the way home. It was O.K. until traffic got real slow, and then I got crabby. It was the only time I didn't earn a dime. I was complaining, "When are we going to be there?" over and over. It sounded like I wanted to know when we'd get home, but what I really meant was, "I'm crabby 'cause this trip is too long. Will you help me?"

Then Mommy helped me. She reached under the seat and pulled out the bubble bottle. She let me put a plastic wand in the bottle and pull it out. Then Mommy took the bubble wand and rolled down the window. I wanted to hold the bubble wand, but Mommy said, "No, you might drop it." Since our car was going so slow, she put the wand out the car window and lots of bubbles flew away. People in other cars smiled and waved, and we waved back. That was fun!

When traffic got back up to reg'lar speed, Mommy put the bubble bottle away. I told her, "That was fun! I hope we get more slow traffic so we can do the bubbles again." Then she said, "I love my sweet girl." We played games the rest of the way home, and I earned a dollar 'cause I was only crabby for that one little bit.

I can't wait until we can go on vacation again, Tommy. I think it's fun. Don't you?

TAKE-AWAY VALUE

Think About It

Help your kids be good by allowing them to earn money for good behavior. I learned this from Dr. Thomas Phelan, author of *1–2–3 Magic*.[5]

Here are some guidelines. Before the trip, decide how much money the kids can earn for every fifteen minutes of good behavior. Each fifteen minutes when the timer beeps, let them know they've earned another dime (or whatever amount you decided upon). Write it down. If you're the only adult in the car, have an older child write it down. If you don't keep a record, the kids may argue that you shortchanged them. Each child is allowed one warning per fifteen minutes. If a child requires a second warning, he or she earns no money for that fifteen minute period.

Here's one more tip. Tell your kids, "You'll get your money as soon as we get the luggage into the hotel." You'll get more help that way.

Talk About It

1. What memories do you have of long trips in the car when you were a child?
2. Do you dread vacation driving because of your child's behavior?
3. How do you help your kids pass the time and overcome boredom on a long trip?
4. What trips might this new approach enable you to take?

Try it

Discuss what steps you'll need to take to use this strategy.

Chapter 14

No, It Isn't!

Tuesday, June 1st

SARAH'S NOT MY friend anymore, Tommy. She used to be my best friend, but not anymore. I'm never going to play with her again!

Sheesh! Sarah kept arguing with me today, and it's her fault. I get along with people as long as they agree with me. But sometimes they say something wrong, and we have an argument 'cause they won't admit I'm right.

The whole thing happened just before Grandma and Grandpa came over this evening. Mommy bought me a brand-new red ball to replace my old one. We came home from the store, and I was playing with it and having lots of fun. But then Sarah came over and tried to grab the ball to play with it. I told her, "It's still my turn 'cause I just got the ball." She said, "It's my turn now 'cause I haven't had a turn with it." I told her, "No, it isn't!" Mommy whispered in my ear, "Lori, you've played with the ball for half an hour, and it's time to share. You can play with your old ball. Or you and Sarah could roll the ball back and forth." But then the phone rang, and Mommy answered it and talked for a long time.

So I kept playing with the ball, and Sarah kept asking me for it. Then she said, "You're mean." I said, "I'm not mean, and you should stop bugging me about having a turn." She shouted, "You're a dummyhead!" I shouted, "No, I'm not! *You're* a dummyhead!" She yelled "I'm not your friend anymore!" Then I yelled, "I'm not *your* friend anymore!" And she went home.

Then I started telling Mommy how mean Sarah was, but Mommy was still on the phone. I said, "I have to talk to you." But she said, "This phone call is very important." I kept trying to tell her about what happened with Sarah, but Mommy said, "Lori, I have two words for you: not now."

Mommy and I argue like that sometimes. She's usually talking to Sarah's mommy and says we'll talk later. She says I shouldn't interrupt her when she's on the phone. But she shouldn't be on the phone when I need to interrupt her.

So Sarah was mean, and Mommy wouldn't talk to me, but I knew what to do. When you're crabby, you have to be crabby at somebody else. I learned that from watching grown-ups. So I was crabby to Rascal and told her, "Go away, and don't bother me."

I went outside, and Jimmy Brodnick was in his front yard. He said, "Where's your dumb dog?" I said, "She's not dumb." Jimmy said, "She is too!" I said, "No, she isn't." Then I said, "Jimmy, I have two words for you: quit bugging me!" He said, "You should go back in the house and play with your stupid dolls." So I told him, "You should play with *your* stupid dolls." He said, "I don't have any." I said, "Yes you do, and I saw them." He said, "Those aren't dolls. Those are action figures." I said, "Action figures *are* dolls." He threw a stick at me, but he missed. Then I went back into our house.

Mommy was off the phone and asked me, "Are you having a hard day?" I nodded. Mommy said, "I'm having a hard day, too." I told her, "Sarah and Jimmy were mean to me." She said, "What happened?" I told her all about Sarah and Jimmy. She hugged me and told me, "The best way to get over a bad day is to cheer someone up. We could both get over being crabby by doing something nice for somebody else, like Grandma and Grandpa."

She asked me, "Should we draw them a picture or write them a note?" Grown-ups always tell us what to do, so when Mommy asked me what to do, that made me feel a little better. When a grown-up gives me a choice, instead of thinking about being crabby and saying, "No," I think about which one I want to choose. I said, "We should do a note and a picture." She said, "That's a great idea." She got out some paper and pens. Mommy wrote for me, and I said,

Dear Grandma and Grandpa,

Are you having a crabby day? Me too. I know how you feel. Is Jimmy being mean to you, too? You are the specialest Grandma and Grandpa in the whole wide world.

Love,

Lori

Then Mommy brought me some paper to draw pictures, but I said, "I don't want paper. I want paper plates." Mommy asked "Why?" I told her, "I want to draw happy pictures on the paper plates 'cause after they eat their yummy food, they're sad 'cause it's gone. But next time, when their food is gone, they'll be happy when they see the pretty pictures I drew on the paper plates." Mommy said, "That's creative. I like it." I drew a picture of a guitar on Grandpa's 'cause he likes music. And I drew a picture of some books on Grandma's 'cause she likes books. Writing to Grandma and Grandpa and drawing pictures for them made me feel a lot better.

Today isn't the only time I argued with Sarah, Tommy. One time, I was at her house, and I wanted to play with her, but she said, "No," 'cause she was reading the Bible. I said, "You don't know how to read." She said, "Yes I do." So I asked, "What are you reading?" She said, "It's Jesus' words." I looked at the page and said, "No it isn't. Jesus talks in red."

Another time, she and I were talking about why the church has a cross on top of the steeple. Sarah said, "It's so people will know it's a church." I said, "No, it isn't." She said, "Then how come there's a cross on top of the steeple?" So I told her, "The cross is there 'cause it's what holds up the church."

Mommy was right. Doing that stuff to cheer up Grandma and Grandpa helped me feel a lot better. I bet Mommy's going to make me apologize to Sarah. I guess I can. I'm not mad anymore. But Sarah said she didn't want to be my friend. What if she is still mad? What if we never get to play together again?

TAKE-AWAY VALUE

Think About It

In this chapter, Lori says "No." Preschoolers say no a lot because they are eager to exercise their independence. Saying no makes them feel like they're making a choice.

You can reduce the frequency of your child saying no by changing the way you tell them to do something. Give them a choice between two options. Lori's mother let her daughter choose between drawing a picture or writing a note (with help) for Grandpa and Grandma. This approach works because kids want to assert their independence by making choices. So offer them choices. Say, "Come to the table for a snack. Which cup do you want to use?" In the morning, ask, "Do you want to wear your blue T-shirt or your red one today?" At the store ask, "Do you want us to buy green beans or corn?" At bedtime ask, "Which book do you want me to read to you?"

If your child says, "No! I don't want to get dressed right now," then you say, "It's time to get dressed. You may choose which T-shirt or I will choose for you." Your child will probably say, in exasperation, "Fine. I'll wear the blue one." If your child still refuses to select a shirt, you should choose which T-shirt the child will wear that day.

Talk About It

1. How would you feel if your spouse or best friend made all the choices for you?
2. When does your child or grandchild say no to you?
3. What do you want your youngster to do?
4. What choices could you offer your child that would meet your goal?

Try It

Give your child some reasonable choices about something he or she needs to do.

Chapter 15

A Dumb Day

Tuesday, June 8th

THIS WAS A dumb day, Tommy, 'cause I had nobody to play with. Sarah is still gone on vacation, and nobody else could play, either. So I sat around like a rump on a log.

Grown-ups don't know how much we love to play. So when they say, "It's time to stop playing and get ready for bed," and we get mad, they think we're being bad. We're usually not being bad. We just really, really love to play, but grown-ups don't understand this 'cause it's been so long since they were kids.

But sometimes I think Mommy and Daddy understand how much I love to play. One time, Mommy and Daddy took me to the City Museum in downtown St. Louis. We played hide-and-seek, and I loved playing with them in the Toddler Town part.

And last Saturday, Daddy took me to the park. It was a lot of fun. When we got to the playground, I looked at Daddy and said, "You can't catch me." That meant he had to chase me. When I ran away, the sand under my shoes made that scrunchy sound. I ran to the slide that's kind of a tube, and I climbed up. I waited at the top of the slide while he climbed up, until he almost got me, and then I slid down headfirst. Then Daddy came down the slide and chased me more. He was part monster, part bear, and part daddy. I was part rabbit, part race car, and all girl. It's my favorite game to play with Daddy 'cause it's funner than anything. And we both know what to do. He has to chase me, and I have to get away. Daddy runs faster and jumps higher, but I have a better grin and I giggle more.

Then something different happened. This one kid asked Daddy to chase him, too. Daddy did. Then more kids wanted to play, and pretty soon Daddy was chasing a lot of kids. It was fun having the other kids play with us, but I wanted Daddy to chase me and not them so much. He's *my* Daddy.

Then I looked around and saw that he was the only adult who played with us. Grown-ups sat on benches and watched him play with their kids. Why didn't those grown-ups play with their own kids? Don't they know how much fun it is?

Our parents know, Tommy. You should see them smile and laugh when they play with me. Playing with them is one of the funnest things ever, for me and for them. Having kids and not playing with them is like getting a brand-new bike in the summer and never riding it! Sheesh!

Here's another thing. When Mommy and Daddy play with me, I'm not so crabby, and it's easier for me to obey them. But Tommy, don't tell grown-ups about this, 'cause then lots of parents will be playing with their kids, and we'll be tricked into being good.

Sometimes Mommy plays "Tickle Tiger" with me. She hides on one side of the house while I sneak from room to room. My heart goes *thumpy-thumpy*, I jump if I hear a noise, and I'm scared to look around the next corner. If she catches me, she gives me a quick tickle. If I get away, I squeal and run back to the living room couch 'cause that's base, and she can't get me there.

And a couple of weeks ago, we had some people from church over to our house. One of the daddies played tag with us. He hardly ever got us 'cause we were fast and smart. He even said so.

Us kids love to play, don't we? Babies like you to play with your fingers, toes, and hair. Big kids, like me, play with our food, and when I see my friend, Sarah, the first thing I say is, "Can you play?"

But talking about playing is making me crabby, 'cause today I had nobody to play with. And what's going to happen when Sarah comes back from vacation? What if I tell her I'm sorry for being mean, and she still doesn't want to be my friend and play with me? What will I do then?

Anyway, playing is one of the most important things about being a kid, 'cause when somebody plays with me, that's how I know they like me. This means when kids ask their parents to play with them, and they do, it's awesomer than anything 'cause it really helps us feel loved. I just wish more grown-ups knew this.

TAKE-AWAY VALUE

Think About It

Since preschoolers love to play, capitalize on this by playing with them. When you play with your child, your child's heart softens toward you, leading him or her to be more obedient. And your heart softens toward your child.

Here are some quick guidelines. First, within reason, let the child choose the activity. Second, be slow to correct your child's strategy or technique. A few suggestions are fine. But too much advice spoils the fun for the child. Third, say lots of encouraging things to your child about the way he or she is playing. Fourth, schedule a time for playing together.

Talk About It

1. How do you feel when someone you love does your favorite activity with you?
2. How will your child feel when you play your child's favorite game just to be together?
3. What does your child love to play?
4. What is the best time of day to play with your child?

Try It

Pick a time to play with your child.

Chapter 16

Help Me

Tuesday, June 15th

I STARTED OUT crabby yesterday. Know why? 'Cause it was boring, and I thought today was never going to come. I wanted today to hurry up and get here 'cause I knew Sarah was coming home from vacation today. So yesterday, I kept asking Mommy, "When will Sarah be home?" Mommy would say, "Today is Monday, and she'll be back tomorrow, which is Tuesday."

I kept asking 'cause I really wanted Sarah to come home, and I couldn't help myself. I wish grown-ups knew that when we ask the same question over and over, it means the feelings are too strong for us to keep them in, and we wish they'd do something to help us feel better.

But Mommy figgered it out and helped me. She smiled, winked at me, and said, "The next time you ask when Sarah's coming home, I'll tickle you." I smiled back at Mommy, tried to wink at her, and went around to the far side of the table. I looked her in the eye. I asked, "When is Sarah coming home?"

Mommy stood up real slow and smiled real big. I giggled, and she said, "Your best friend, Sarah, will come back ON TICKLE TUESDAY!" All of a sudden she chased me around and around the table and hollered, "I'm going to tickle you to smithereens!" I squealed and ran, but all of a sudden, she stopped and ran the other way around the table. I couldn't stop, and she grabbed me. I squealed again, she tickled me a little bit, and we hugged each other.

Then I felt way better. Us kids live in our feelings, and when parents help us with our feelings, it's great. It's like a TV show about hummingbirds I watched with Daddy. The 'nnouncer said hummingbirds use up lots of energy moving their wings back and forth real fast, and they have to eat a lot to get their energy back. That's how kids are. We use lots of energy on our feelings, and we need a lot of help to get our good feelings back.

Parents can help us with our feelings by playing a fun game with us, like when Mommy chased and tickled me. Here's another way. When parents see us do something good, they can say "Good job," "I like your smile," or "Thank you for staying in your chair during dinner." That makes us feel good and you know what? When we feel good, we act good, too. Parents know we're naughty when we're crabby, but I'm not sure they know that if they help us feel happy, we'll obey a lot more.

Anyway, yesterday Mommy helped me by chasing and tickling me. Today, she helped me with my feelings in some different ways. It was finally Tuesday, and I couldn't wait for Sarah to get home, but I was scared 'cause I knew I had to apologize to her. And I thought she wouldn't want to be my friend anymore.

This morning, after breakfast, Mommy helped me with my feelings. She made up a pretending game. She put her finger to her lips and whispered, "We're going to pretend there's a big cat sleeping in the house, and you and I are little mice. We have to sneak down to the basement, bring up the laundry, and put it away before the cat wakes up." So we tiptoed down the stairs. When the stair creaked, it was scary and fun. We got the laundry and came back upstairs. Mommy went up first. At the top of the stairs she looked for the cat. The coast was clear, so she waved for me to come up, too. We put the laundry away, and it was fun 'cause we were super quiet and that pretend cat never woke up.

Then Mommy did another thing to help me with me feelings. She took me into the living room, and we sat on the blue chair where Grandma sits when she reads to me. Mommy said, "I have some exciting news. You get to be the flower girl in a wedding. A flower girl wears a pretty dress and gets to be in the wedding. Another girl was going to be the flower girl, but she broke her leg, and the people getting married want you to be the flower girl. It'll be fun because weddings are beautiful, and you'll get a new dress." That made me feel good 'cause being in a wedding sounds fun.

I played for the rest of the morning and, in the afternoon, Mommy let me watch the movie, *Cinderella.*[6] I loved it! The mean sisters reminded me of Jimmy Brodnick.

After the movie was over, she helped me again. She told me what to say to apologize to Sarah. Some grown-ups tell their kids to apologize, and the kids say no. The grown-ups get mad at the kids for disobeying, but the kids say, no 'cause they don't know how to apologize.

For the rest of the afternoon, I looked outside a lot to see if Sarah was back yet. I worried that she would get lost and not come home today. Or maybe she would still be mad and maybe I would never, ever have a friend like Sarah to play with.

Then I heard a car door shut, and I ran outside, but it was only Daddy. He asked, "Where's my hug?" I told him, "You're not getting one, 'cause you're supposed to be Sarah."

A couple of minutes later, I heard more car doors shut, and this time it was Sarah and her family in their driveway next door. Mommy came outside too, and handed Teddy Bear to me. It felt good to hug him tight. Mommy told Sarah, "Lori has something to say to you." It got real quiet, and everybody looked at me and waited for me to talk. My heart went *thumpy-thumpy*. Mommy whispered the first couple of words in my ear, and that got me started. I told Sarah, "I'm sorry for being crabby at you and not sharing my ball." She said, "OK. Hey, look at this new T-shirt I got on vacation." Then Mommy asked, "May Sarah come over to our house to play?" Her parents said yes.

I only got to play with Sarah a little bit, 'cause pretty soon, it was time for Grandma and Grandpa to come over, so Sarah had to go home. But that's OK, 'cause Mommy's going to take me shopping and buy me a beautiful new flower girl dress. And I know what kind I want. I want one just like Cinderella's.

TAKE-AWAY VALUE

Think About It

In this chapter, Lori and her mother pretended they were mice who had to sneak past a sleeping cat. Your preschooler possesses a vivid imagination. Utilize it to make everyday experiences more enjoyable.

When driving to the grocery store, say, "Let's pretend we're in a spaceship going to Mars." Or you could suggest, "Let's imagine we're in a horse-drawn carriage clip-clopping to the castle." When cleaning the living room, say, "Uh-oh. (Winking) I think there's a big sleeping bear on the couch. Do you think we can finish cleaning before he wakes up?" Spice things up with an occasional growl as the bear rolls over in its sleep. When it's time to go back in the house after playing, say, "Everybody gets to be a car or truck. It's time to drive yourself back into the house. I'm going to be a big truck. *BEEP! BEEP!* What are you going to be?"

Talk About It

1. As an adult, what novel or movie captured your imagination?
2. When is your child entertained by what he or she imagines?
3. What have you done to utilize your child's imagination to help him or her be good?
4. What else could you do to tap into your child's imagination?

Try It

Use your imagination when interacting with your preschooler.

Chapter 17

The Big Purchase

Tuesday, June 22nd

TODAY STARTED OUT great, but it didn't stay that way. At breakfast, Mommy said, "I have a surprise for you, and I'll tell you all about it when you start eating."

As soon as I started eating, she said, "Princess Loreli, we're going to the store today." I asked, "Is it for my dress?" She said, "Yes." I was so excited, I jumped out of my chair and ran around the table. Mommy said, "I'm glad you're excited, but eat your cereal, so we can get ready and go to the store."

After breakfast, I got dressed. Then Mommy drove you and me to the store. On the way, she said, "Let's go over the shopping rules. The rules are:

1. Stay with Mommy.
2. Ask before you touch.
3. Mommy decides what we buy."

Sometimes, when we're on our way to buy groceries at Schnucks, she'll say, "Try to say all three rules before we go past the next traffic light." That makes it fun. And I like it when her rules tell me what to do instead of what not to do. Mommy calls these "yes rules." A "yes rule" is like "stay with Mommy." A "no rule" is like "don't run in the store." Lots of grown-ups have "no rules," like "don't hit." But they should change that to a "yes rule," like "keep your hands to yourself."

"No rules" are dumb, 'cause a rule like "don't run in the store," makes me think about running. Us kids get stuck in our thoughts a lot. If we think about the "no rule," we get stuck thinking about being bad. And when we keep thinking about being bad, we do bad things. But when the "yes rules" get us thinking about being good, we do good things.

Anyway, after we got to the store, Mommy told the store lady about my dress. But the store didn't have any dresses. All it had was stuff you make dresses out of. Mommy said, "It's a fabric store, and they sell the material to make dresses." So I was crabby, since I thought I was getting my new dress today.

And I was crabby 'cause I want a dress like Cinderella's, 'cause then I'd feel beautiful. But Mommy said, "Lori, your dress will be beautiful." I told her, "If you buy me a dress like Cinderella's, I'll always be good." Mommy said, "I expect you to be good whether or not you get what you want. Another thing is that it's not up to me what dress you wear. The bride chose the dresses for this wedding."

I told Mommy, "We should let her watch our Cinderella movie. Then she'll want me to wear one like that, too." Mommy said, "Your new dress will be very pretty. You'll see." Then Mommy and the store lady talked. The store lady said, "We don't have the material for your dress. But we can order it, and it'll come in next week."

Mommy told me, "It will be OK. The wedding is in three weeks. And the material will come in next week." But I wanted to wear the dress today and pretend to be Cinderella. Even if it doesn't look like Cinderella's dress, I could pretend. But now all my pretending is ruined 'cause of that dumb store! Sheesh! When we got in the car, I said, "I hate that store. I was supposed to get my dress but I didn't. I want some candy! NOW!"

Mommy talked to me in a quiet voice, but it was strong, too. She said, "It's OK to be upset about not getting your dress. It's not OK to be rude to me. We're going to Sarah's birthday party now. You have a choice. If you stop complaining, I'll keep driving, and we'll get to the party in a few minutes. If you keep being angry and rude, I'll pull the car over until you stop being rude. If I have to pull over, you will be late for your party. You decide."

I decided to be quiet. Mommy was quiet too and that helped. Some grown-ups talk to us to help us not be mad. It works better when they're quiet. That helps me get quiet with my mouth, and way down inside too.

On the way to the party, we dropped you off to spend the afternoon with Grandma at her house, 'cause she didn't work at the library today. Then Mommy and I went to the party.

It was at a new restaurant called The Firehouse. It was so much fun, Tommy! It looks like a fire station, and they cook everything over a wood fire. They can cook pizza and burgers for the kids and grilled chicken and steak for grown-ups.

The people who work there wear firefighter outfits and red firefighter hats. I got a red paper firefighter's hat to wear and keep, just like all the kids. There's a big, wood fire engine in the middle of the restaurant, and we played on it while we waited for our food.

Then the food came. The kids all had pizza, and after we ate it, you should have seen what the waiters did. Some waiters slid down the pole in the middle of the restaurant while red lights flashed and a siren played. Some other waiters ran over to our table with the cake. They lit the candles on the cake and told us kids to grab this hose thingy. The waiter turned it on and instead of water coming out, it squirted air. We moved it back and forth, and it blew out the candles. Then everybody clapped, and we ate the cake. It was yummy!

The Firehouse Restaurant was a lot of fun, but on the way home, I thought real hard about my dress. What if the store doesn't get the stuff for my dress next week? Then I won't get to be in the wedding and everything will be ruined. You're lucky, Tommy, 'cause you don't know how hard it is not to be little anymore.

TAKE-AWAY VALUE

Think About It

When you shop with your youngster, make a short list of rules and tell them to your child. State the rules positively. Positive rules tell children what they should do rather than what they shouldn't do.

The rules will depend on your child's tendencies. Think of their misbehavior, then translate those behaviors into positive behavior. If your child screams in the store, the rule is, "Use your inside voice." If your child pokes a sibling, the rule is "Keep your hands to yourself." If your child grabs merchandise while riding in the shopping cart, the rule is, "Keep your hands inside the cart."

It also helps to offer an incentive. Before you go into the store, offer a small reward, such as a piece of candy. If offering candy bothers you, offer a different reward. If your child is naughty, give one warning. If your child persists, he or she doesn't get the reward.

Talk About It

1. Where do you shop with your child?
2. What bad behavior does your child engage in while shopping?
3. What are your expectations for your kids when they are shopping?
4. How would you express those expectations as positively stated rules?

Try it

Make your shopping rules and tell your child.

Chapter 18

Uh-Oh

Tuesday, June 29

I DID AN "Uh-oh" thing today, Tommy. This morning, I asked, "Mommy, will you play a game with me?" She said "Yes," but then she got a phone call. She talked a long time, and I got bored. So I got some markers and some paper, and I drew a picture of our house. Then I wanted to draw a way bigger picture.

So I took the markers into my bedroom and drew a big picture on the wall by my bed. I drew our house, Sarah's house, and all the houses on our block. And I put an extra house on the block for Grandma and Grandpa 'cause I wish they lived on our block, too.

When Mommy finished on the phone, she came into my room. She looked at the picture I drew on the wall. I said, "Uh-oh." It got real quiet, and my heart went *thumpy-thumpy*.

Mommy said, "Tell me about the picture on the wall." I said, "I wanted to draw a bigger picture of all the houses on our block." Mommy said, "The rule is you only color on paper. Or you can do it on paper plates if you get permission. You won't get to use the markers for a week, and you have to clean the picture off the wall." She brought some rags and wall cleaner stuff. She said, "When it's all cleaned off, you may play again." She stayed in the room to watch and a couple of times she said, "You are doing a good job, Lori." I had to rub the wall hard for a long time to get the marker off.

It's like the story in the Bible, where Daniel worked for a king. They had a party and stuff, and then the king got scared when a hand wrote on the wall. The king said, "Uh-oh," 'cause he knew you get in big trouble for writing on the wall. Then Daniel said, "Yep. You're in big trouble, and you don't get to be king anymore." So *don't* write on the wall, Tommy.

Right after I finished cleaning the wall, Mommy got a call from the store where we ordered the material for my dress. They said it came in, so we drove to the store to get it. When we were driving there, I told Mommy, "I hope the store lady made a mistake, and the material they got was for a Cinderella dress." Mommy didn't say anything about that. She said, "Tell me the three shopping rules." After I said them, she said, "You did such a good job saying the rules that we get to play a game in the store."

She said, "It's called the 'thank you game.' We'll count how many times we say thank you, and if we say it five times, we win!" On the way into the store, a lady let us go through the door ahead of her, so Mommy said "Thank you." That was our first thank you, so Mommy winked at me and held up one finger.

Then we went to the counter to talk to the store lady. Mommy said, "Thank you for calling us and telling us the material is here." Mommy winked at me again, and held up two fingers. Then I whispered to Mommy, "I want a turn to say thank you," and she whispered an idea into my ear. So after Mommy paid the lady for the material, I said, "Thank you for helping us." I tried to wink at Mommy, and I held up three fingers. Then the lady said, "You are a polite young lady." I said "thank you" again. Mommy and I started to walk out of the store, and we both held up four fingers.

Mommy said to me, "Uh-oh, we only said 'thank you' four times, and it's time to leave the store." I said, "Call Daddy on your cell phone, and let me thank him for letting me be a flower girl." She called Daddy, and I thanked him. He said, "You're welcome, Princess Loreli." He was busy and couldn't talk more, so we said good-bye.

I tried to wink at Mommy, and I held up five fingers. In the parking lot, she gave me a high five 'cause we gave five thank you's. I like saying thank you when it's fun.

After we got home, Mommy was on the phone again. She was talking quiet, and I wanted to hear what she was saying. So I played with my red rubber ball and rolled it closer, so I could hear what she was saying. She couldn't see me 'cause I was behind the counter that sticks out into the kitchen. She was talking to Sarah's Mommy. She said, "Lori colored on the wall today. I didn't yell at her. I just made her clean it up. I used to holler, but then Lori would holler back."

Mommy's smart, Tommy, 'cause now instead of hollering back at her, it gets me thinking that I don't want to color on the wall again 'cause it's hard to clean it off. It's like what happened that one time. I took all those big books off the shelf in the living room, so I could see the pictures. I sat on the floor and looked at them until the doorbell rang. It was Sarah and she wanted to play. I asked Mommy, "Can I play?" She said, "You may play as soon as you put the books back on the shelf." Those books were heavy. I put them away, and I'll tell you one thing, Tommy. I'm never going to take down all those books again.

Anyway, Mommy says stuff to me like, "If you mess it up, clean it up." And she told Sarah's Mommy, "When the consequences do the preaching, it's a sermon kids remember." I don't know what that means, but I do know one thing. Sometimes it's not so much fun having a smart Mommy.

TAKE-AWAY VALUE

Think About It

This chapter illustrates the natural consequences approach to discipline. It lets children experience the results of their actions. That's why Lori had to clean the wall after she drew on it and put the books away after taking out so many.

Sometimes it's hard to figure out the natural consequences. Two guidelines will help. First, if the child abuses a privilege, he or she loses the privilege. So if your son gets into a fight with a friend, what privilege was abused? Playing with a buddy is a privilege, so your youngster loses that privilege for a day or so. If your daughter acts ornery about picking up the toys, she loses the privilege of playing with those toys for a while.

The second guideline is that if the child messes it up, he or she should clean it up. When I was young, I scribbled on the pew at church once. But I only did it once, because my mother made me clean it off.

Talk About It

1. As an adult, what did you learn through suffering the consequences? For example, did you learn to keep track of your keys because you lost them?
2. What bad behavior does your child engage in?
3. Is this naughty behavior an example of abusing a privilege or messing something up?
4. Brainstorm a natural consequence to apply to that bad behavior.

Try it

Use the natural consequence you just figured out.

Chapter 19

Yummy!

Tuesday, July 6th

GRANDPA JUST WENT to the bathroom, and Grandma is looking for a book to read to me 'cause she thinks you're still sleeping. If I hurry, I can talk to you for a little bit.

Did you like the picnic on Sunday? It was on the Fourth of July, and we had a big picnic in Tower Grove Park. They put food on tables in the shelter. And they hung up American flags and red, white, and blue stuff. I figgered it out. They put up the flags and stuff 'cause it was the Fourth of July, and we celebrated the Decoration of Independence.

When it was time to eat, Mommy fed you, and Grandpa helped me get my food. He said, "Wow! What a great buffet!" I asked him, "What's a buffet?" He said, "It means there's more food than you can shake a stick at." I asked, "How come there is so much food?" He winked at me and said, "Church people like to eat 'cause Jesus said, 'Wherever two or three are gathered in my name, there will be a hot dish and a Jello™ salad.'"

By the time Mommy finished feeding you, I was done eating. She asked, "Do you want more green beans?" I said, "No. I'm full." A little later, I said, "I want some cake." Mommy asked me, "How come you were full two minutes ago, but now you have room?" I told her, "I have room for dessert 'cause the cake goes in a different part of the tummy than the green beans. The green beans part is small, but the cake part is very big, so I have plenty of room for cake."

Kids know that our tummies have different areas. That's why we don't like having our food mixed together on our plate. Grown-ups tell us not to worry if our food gets mixed together on our plate, 'cause it all goes to the same place. But that's wrong, Tommy. Different foods go to different parts of the tummy.

Us kids don't like food mixed together 'cause it's hard for our tummies to put the different foods where they are supposed to go. But grown-ups make us eat mixed food, and that's why we get so many tummy aches.

But grown-ups have forgotten this, so they eat lots of food that's mixed together, like stir-fry and salad. Yuck! Eating mixed-up food is bad for their tummies, too. It hurts their tummies and makes them swell. That's why so many grown-ups are trying to make their tummies smaller.

Anyway, I wanted some cake, but Grandpa said I should try a root beer float. He said, "It's root beer with a scoop of ice cream." It looked funny, and I didn't want to try it. And it's mixed food. But Grandpa said, "It tastes Wonderful, with a capital W!" He said, "Just try a little." So I tried it. I was afraid it would taste yucky, but you know what? It was good. It tasted almost as good as cookies.

Then Grandpa said, "If you have a snack or a dessert with somebody, that makes you snack buddies." That means that he and I are snack buddies! And he said, "Snack buddies like to try new foods." I wanted more, so I went up to the food table with him and got my own root beer float. It was yummy, with a capital W! I love being snack buddies with Grandpa.

Sometimes I don't like food if it looks yucky or it tastes yucky. But then sometimes I like it if it's fun. I like the food Mommy cooks 'cause she makes it fun. Sometimes we have a Cinderella meal. I get to be Cinderella, we pretend Rascal is a mean stepsister, and Mommy is the fairy godmother. I eat lots of food, and I'm not fussy 'cause it's so much fun.

And another time eating was fun was at Sarah's house when she ate a baked potato. I didn't used to like them, but when Sarah started eating her baked potato, I could tell it was yummy, and then I wanted one, too. And you know what? Sarah was right! And now I like baked potatoes, even at our house. It's like this, Tommy. You know how when one kid really wants a toy, the other kids want it too? It's the same way with food. When one kid eats something and likes it, the other kids will probably like it too. That's 'cause for kids, our feelings have a lot to do with how we eat.

Oh, I almost forgot to tell you. Do you remember how Grandma's been working on my dress for the wedding? It's almost done, and tomorrow,

I'll get to try it on. I can't wait! It's going to be pretty, and when I wear it, I'll be pretty too. You'll see. And the wedding is next week. I can't wait for that either!

I hear Grandpa coming. It's time for my snack, and I'm hungry. I want to be snack buddies with Grandpa, and I'm going to tell him there's lots of room in the root beer float part of my tummy.

TAKE-AWAY VALUE

Think About It

In earlier chapters, Lori explained that feelings drive preschoolers. That includes their food likes and dislikes. That's why saying, "Eat it. It's good for you," rarely motivates kids to eat because it doesn't connect with their emotions. In contrast, look at cereal marketed to kids. The pictures on the cereal boxes make the food look like fun.

Use your child's feelings to get him or her to eat healthy food. How? Give a ho-hum food a clever name based on your child's interests. Don't offer ordinary food. Instead, serve "Cinderella's Tea " or "Rodeo Ravioli." Or you could create a meal based on your child's favorite movie or book. Use a few simple decorations, and give the food and utensils names that fit in your child's story. If your child loves a story about a princess, set the table with "Princess Knives and Forks" and serve "Castle Casserole." If your youngster loves a movie about outer space, serve "Astronaut Apples" and let your child wear a "gravity belt" to keep him from floating away from the table.

Talk About It

1. What foods did you dislike as a child?
2. What food does your child dislike?
3. What strategies have you used to get your child to eat well?
4. What toys and stories fascinate your child?

Try It

Use the ideas above to prepare and serve food with its new name.

Chapter 20

The Bride and the Goon

Tuesday, July 13th

YOU SHOULD'VE SEEN the wedding on Saturday, Tommy. I've been busy, and I haven't had time to talk to you about it. On Saturday morning, I ate breakfast and played in my room with Teddy Bear. We pretended he was getting married. His paws were shaking, so I told him not to be scared and that he looked very handsome.

Then I had to get ready, so I took a bath and put on my new dress. It was beautiful! Mommy brushed my hair and braided part of it.

On the way to church, Mommy told me, "The wedding will be like the rehearsal. You'll walk down the aisle the same way, but there will be a lot more people in the church. You don't have to be nervous because the people at the wedding will be very nice." It helps when grown-ups tell me what's going to happen.

Anyway, we got to the church at noon thirty, way before the wedding started, 'cause I was part of the wedding party. I didn't know why they called it a "wedding party." But I figgered it out. They call it a wedding party since people bring presents, and we all get cake.

After a while, a lot of people came into the church. They were all dressed up and sat down in the big room with all the pews. Then everybody in the wedding party lined up. Miss Jan was right in front of me. I got to be her special helper during the rehearsal, and she was nice. When we were lined up, she said, "You'll do a good job, and the wedding will be fun." She was mostly right.

Then it was time to walk down the aisle. The ladies went first, one at a time. The ring bear went, and then it was my turn. My heart went *thumpy-thumpy*, my mouth was dry, and when everyone looked at me, I froze. When I saw Mommy and Daddy smiling at me, I remembered I had to walk to the front, so I did.

Then it was the bride's turn. The music got loud and everyone stood. She goes last 'cause she's the most important. But I'm pretty important 'cause I came right before her.

When the bride got down to the front, the preacher said, "We are gathered together to join two people together in holy macaroni." Then he said all the people could sit down. After that, some people sang some songs and read some stuff. And the people getting married lit candles and prayed.

The preacher got up again and said, "Marriage is appointed by God." He said a bunch of other things, but my ears got tired, so I stopped listening. And when he kept on talking a long time, my legs got real tired too, so I sat down. Some grown-ups laughed.

Miss Jan was standing near me. She bent over, smiled, and whispered "Are you OK?" I told her, "No. My legs are tired, and the preacher is talking too long." She was holding flowers but had some mints in her hand, too. She gave me two mints and said, "These will give you energy to stand up." So I put them in my mouth, and I stood up. I think the preacher figgered out he was talking too much, 'cause he only said a little bit more.

After the wedding, we drove to the Botanical Garden for the reception. They had a fountain with chocolate syrup in it. People put strawberries on a toothpick and held them under the fountain and got chocolate-covered strawberries. I did it too, and it was yummy. Then I wanted to put some of my sandwich in the fountain, but Mommy said it wouldn't taste good. So I told her Grandpa taught me that snack buddies like to try new foods.

So she said, "If you eat most of your turkey sandwich, you may put some of the chocolate syrup in a cup and dip the last bite of your sandwich in the chocolate." So that's what I did, and Mommy was right. It was yucky, with a capital W!

On the way home, Mommy asked me "What did you think of the wedding?" I said, "It was fun, except the preacher talked too long and my legs got tired." Daddy asked me, "Do you have any questions?" I asked him, "Why did the bride wear a white dress?" He said, "It's to show that it's the happiest day of her life." Then I asked, "So then why did the man wear black?" He laughed hard and said, "That's a good one!" Then he said, “It’s ’cause grown-ups dress up for important occasions and wearing black is very dressy.” Then we got home. I ate supper, played with Sarah, and went to bed.

I’m glad I was in the wedding, Tommy. I liked dressing up and stuff. I just wonder what’s going to happen next.

TAKE-AWAY VALUE

Think About It

Rewards provide a strong motive for behavior. So instead of giving a privilege outright, offer it after your youngster obeys. Lori's mother did this by letting Lori dip her sandwich in the chocolate syrup after she ate her turkey sandwich.

Here are a few ways you can use this. Say, "You may play as soon as you take your dishes over to the sink." Tell your child, "I'll turn the movie on as soon as you put the toys away." Say, "We'll go to the park after you help me walk the dog."

This approach works best when you state it positively. An example of a positive statement is, "I'll invite your friend over to play as soon as you put the books away." The negative version would be, "I won't invite your friend over to play until you put the books away."

Do children have to earn everything? No. But this strategy is very appropriate if they have an unfinished chore. It will motivate them to complete it.

Talk About It

1. When did you motivate yourself to complete an unpleasant task by promising yourself a reward?
2. Describe your motivation level when you're promised a reward for doing a chore.
3. What does your child love to do?
4. What could you motivate your child to do in order to earn a cherished privilege?

Try it

Use this approach with your child.

Chapter 21

Grandpa's Secret

Tuesday, July 20th

GUESS WHAT I did today? I played a whole bunch of brand-new games and stuff. Right after breakfast, Mommy started a new game with me. She took out the little red and white tape recorder that I can use. She said, "Lori, when you're good, I'll tell Daddy about it on the tape. When he gets home, he'll listen to it." So when I got dressed, she turned on the tape recorder and said, "Daddy, Lori did a great job getting dressed." Then we cleaned the house. Mommy kept turning on the tape recorder and telling Daddy stuff. She'd say, "Lori put her clean laundry away." I got to say stuff into the tape recorder too. I like being good when it's fun, Tommy.

But I argued with Mommy one time. After lunch, she said, "I need you to play quietly so I can pay some bills and so you won't wake Tommy. You may play with Teddy Bear, look through some books, or play quietly for fifteen minutes." I said, "I don't want to be quiet!" She said, "Play quietly." Then she walked away.

I was going to argue more, but I couldn't 'cause there was nobody to argue with. When we're young, our feelings are the boss of us. We get stuck in our feelings, and when grown-ups argue with us, we *really* get stuck in our feelings.

But Mommy told me what to do and walked away. Since there was nobody to argue with, I stopped thinking about arguing, and I started thinking about playing. I read *Cinderella* to Teddy Bear. I know all the words 'cause Grandma has read it to me so much. And since Teddy sat still, I let him turn the pages and point to the pictures.

Pretty soon, you woke up, Mommy was done paying bills, and she said, "Good job playing quietly, Lori. Tommy's awake now, so you don't have to be quiet." She turned on the tape recorder and told Daddy, "Lori was quiet so Tommy could sleep and I could pay bills. I'm proud of her." Then it was my turn. I said, "Hi, Daddy. Teddy Bear was good, too. But he doesn't want to talk on the tape recorder 'cause he only talks to me."

Then Mommy told me we're going to have a neighborhood party in about a month. There will be lots of food, a clown, and games for the kids. There's going to be a race for the kids and every kid who runs will get a coupon for a free hamburger at The Firehouse Restaurant. Yummy! I love that restaurant!

When Daddy came home, we played the tape for him. He hugged me and said, "I'm proud of you, Lori!" Then he changed his clothes and did some exercises. I did some too. He did some sit-ups, lifted his shirt a little, smiled, and asked, "Do I have six-pack abs?" I said, "What's that?" He said, "It means I have lots of muscles in my stomach." I said, "I guess."

Then he asked Mommy, "Do I have six pack abs?" She looked at his tummy, smiled, and said, "It's more like a two liter bottle." He grinned and told Mommy, "I'm going to tickle you!" So she ran, and Daddy was laughing when he chased her.

He caught her and tickled her, but not very much. They were laughing a lot, and Mommy hollered, "Save me, Lori! Daddy has turned into the Tickle Monster." I ran over and tickled Daddy, but he's not ticklish. Mommy said, "The only way to stop the Tickle Monster is if we both hug him at the same time." So we did, and the Tickle Monster turned back into Daddy. Then I told Mommy, "Tease Daddy so we can play the tickle game again." She said, "No, I'm tired from laughing so much."

A little later, Grandma and Grandpa came over. I told them about the block party and the race. Grandpa said, "That sounds like fun. We could go outside and practice for the race." I said, "OK."

I went outside and waited for Grandpa. Jimmy Brodnick was in his front yard and he asked me what I was doing. I told him, "I'm waiting for my Grandpa 'cause he's going to run with me. We're going to practice running for the race at the block party." Jimmy said, "I'll beat you in that race 'cause boys are way better than girls, and girls are dumb."

Before I could say anything back to him, Grandpa came outside and said, "I'll race you to the corner, Lori!" We ran all the way. I got tired, but I still beat Grandpa by a little bit.

Then it was time for supper, and we had grilled cheese sandwiches. Grandpa asked me, "Why don't you eat the crusts?" I said, "I don't like them." He said, "I have a secret for you. Eating crusts helps you run faster." I told Grandpa, "Sarah is a fast runner, and she doesn't eat her crusts." Grandpa said, "Just think how much faster she would run if she ate her crusts." I asked, "If I eat my crusts, will that help me beat Jimmy Brodnick in the race?" Grandpa said, "If you eat your crusts and practice running every day, you'll have a good chance." So I ate a little bit of one of the crusts.

After supper, Grandma read *Cinderella* to me twice. Then I told Grandpa I wanted to practice running again. I raced him to the corner, and this time I beat him by a lot. The crusts worked! Tommy, maybe if you started eating crusts, you'd learn to walk.

When we got back in the house, Grandpa went down to the basement to get something. On his way up the stairs, he twisted his knee and yelled, "Ow!" It took him a long time to get back up the stairs. Grandma helped him to the couch and put a small bag of ice on his knee. I wanted to help Grandpa feel better, so I hugged him, and said, "Grandpa, I promise I'll keep eating my crusts and practicing running." He smiled.

I just hope his knee will be OK.

TAKE-AWAY VALUE

Think About It

It's hard to resist arguing with your preschooler when he or she says things that are obviously wrong. Lori objected when her mother told her to play quietly. Her mother wisely remained firm but calm and avoided arguing with her.

Arguing with your defiant child only makes the aggravation worse, like itching a mosquito bite. But when you remain calm, the focus stays on your child's or grandchild's compliance.

Avoid arguing by telling your child what to do, and then walk away. Walking away takes away the opportunity for your child to argue because there's no one to argue with. Walking away also conveys that your words are powerful and should be obeyed.

If the confrontation requires some compliance, such as turning off the television, approach things a little differently. Say, "You need to turn off the TV and put your shoes on. If I have to come back and turn it off, there will be no more movies or television today." Then walk away. Be sure to check on your child in a few minutes and carry out any consequences you mentioned if they are needed.

Talk About It

1. Describe a recent incident when you were angry at someone.
2. When you were angry, how open were you to an opposing point of view?
3. When does your child angrily object to something you tell him or her to do?
4. What makes it hard for you to keep calm when your child argues with you?

Try It

Plan your response for the next time your child acts defiantly or argues.

Chapter 22

No Grandma and Grandpa

Tuesday, July 27th

BAD NEWS, TOMMY. Grandma and Grandpa aren't coming over tonight. Grandpa hurt his knee again. Remember when he hurt it last week? He twisted it again this morning stepping off the front porch at his house. His knee hurt a lot, so Grandma took him to the emergency room. He's got to have surgery in a couple of days. Sheesh! Now Grandpa won't be able to run with me to help me practice for that race at the neighborhood party.

So Grandpa's resting at his house tonight, and Grandma's taking care of him. Mommy said he has to have surgery now so he can be ready to teach when school starts. He's a music teacher at the elementary school.

I know a lot about music 'cause Mommy told me all about it. She's Grandpa and Grandma's daughter, you know. She learned a lot about music from Grandpa.

I love singing. On Sunday, on the way home from church, I sang along with a CD that was playing "Jesus Loves Me." I sang real loud. Do you remember? Daddy said, "Lori, why are you singing at the top of your lungs?" I said, "If I sing loud enough, the devil will go to his room, shut the door, and put pillows over his ears so he can't hear me sing. If he's doing that, he can't get people to do bad stuff." Then Daddy sang with me.

I like the song "London Britches Falling Down," and I like "Old MacDonald." It goes like this:

Old MacDonald had a farm
And Bingo was his name-o.

Singing is fun, but so is listening to music. Mommy taught me all about classical music. She told me about Chy Kopsky and Johann Sebastian Rockmaninov. I like classical music 'cause I dance to it. And I dance when we watch the movie *Fantasia* 'cause it's got good music.

Sometimes on Saturday mornings, Mommy and I eat breakfast in our jammies. Then we put on our bathrobes, and we dance to music. We call it "bathrobe ballet." We dance around the living room, and Mommy's teaching me to be graceful.

This Saturday morning we did bathrobe ballet. It was fun! Mommy played that one real fast part of *The Nutcracker Sweet*. We both danced, and we were pretty awesome. And I wasn't the only one who thought so. Mommy forgot to shut the drapes, and when we finished the song, that one family that lives down the block was standing on our sidewalk, watching us, and clapping. I took a bow, but Mommy's face got red, and she ran out of the living room.

Sometimes I don't dance when the music plays. Like this one time, a long time ago, when I was little, Mommy says I was scared of thunder boomers. So Daddy played a CD of the 1812 overture. That's the one with cannons in it. He played the part where the cannons were shooting, walked to the window, and talked to the storm. He said, "You better go away, or Lori and I will shoot you with our music." The storm didn't listen to Daddy, so we shot at it with the cannons in the music. After a while, that storm went away 'cause it was scared of us, and Daddy gave me a high five. We still play that game sometimes when a storm comes, but it's just for fun, and I'm not scared of the storms anymore.

One time Jimmy Brodnick told me, "Classical music is dumb, and it's for babies." I told him, "You better be quiet 'cause classical music is awesome. I know all about it 'cause my Grandpa is a music teacher. And he told me the only time most people hear classical music is when somebody's cell phone rings."

Anyway, since Grandma and Grandpa couldn't come tonight, Mommy called them so I could talk to them. Grandma said, "I got some more books for you from the library, and I can't wait to read them to you." She said, "I love you, Lori." And I said, "I love you, Grandma."

Then I talked to Grandpa. I told him, "Don't worry. I'm still eating my crusts and practicing running for the race. Sometimes Daddy takes me to Forest Park so I can run on the bike path." And I sang him a song to cheer Grandpa up. I made it up right then, and I sang,

"Once there was a little frog,
who liked to hop around,
and he swam and played with his friends,
and he had fun."

Grandpa said he liked that song. I asked Grandpa if he'd make up a song for me. Grandpa said, "I'm glad you can make up a song so quickly. It takes me a long time to write a song." I said, "If you could make up a song for me, then we could be snack buddies *and* song buddies." He said, "That sounds like a lot of fun, but I'll have to think about that. I can't make up a song right now. I love you, Lori." And I said, "I love you too, Grandpa." And we said good-bye.

I sure hope the doctor can help Grandpa's knee to be OK. And I hope Grandpa will write me a song. I wonder what it will be like.

TAKE-AWAY VALUE

Think About It

Lori described how her father helped her overcome her fear of thunderstorms by "shooting" them. When feelings overwhelm your child, coach your child to do something in response. Suggesting a response gives your youngster a chance to strike back and regain control of his or her emotions.

Here are some examples. If your preschooler feels jealous of the time you give to your baby, let your preschooler draw pictures to help decorate the baby's room. Let him or her decorate one T-shirt for the baby and another one for himself or herself.

If your child experiences a meltdown when it's time to end play time at the park, encourage your youngster to say "good-bye" to the park. It could be something like, "Good-bye park. I'll come back as soon as I can."

Talk About It

1. Tell a story about a time when you felt upset. What did you do to cope?
2. When someone gives a helpful suggestion about how to cope with your feelings, how does that make you feel toward that person?
3. What makes your child upset or afraid?
4. What action(s) could you encourage your child to take to cope with the feelings?

Try It

Choose something your child can do the next time he or she feels afraid.

Chapter 23

Will Grandpa Be OK?

Tuesday, August 3rd

I WAS WORRIED about Grandpa last week. Remember last week when we visited him in the hospital? It was after he had surgery on his knee.

When it was time to go see him, I cried, hugged Mommy tight, and said, "I don't want Grandpa to die." Mommy asked, "Why do you think he will die?" I said, "One time, Daddy watched the news, and this one guy died after surgery." Mommy said, "Grandpa's not going to die. He didn't have that kind of surgery. His knee is already starting to heal. But it still hurts a lot, and he needs us to cheer him up by visiting him."

I stopped crying, and I tried to think of how we could cheer up Grandpa. Then I figgered it out. But I didn't want Mommy to know what I was going to do. So I waited until she was on the phone 'cause that's when she doesn't watch me as close. I knew I wouldn't have to wait long, and I was right!

A couple of minutes later, when somebody called, I went into the kitchen and grabbed a plastic knife we brought home from The Firehouse Restaurant. I used it to cut some food. My heart went *thumpy-thumpy* 'cause I didn't want Mommy to find out what I was doing. When I was done, I put the food in my little purse and put the knife away. There were some crumbs, so I put a napkin over them so Mommy wouldn't see them.

When she got off the phone, we got in the car and went to the hospital. My heart was still going *thumpy-thumpy* 'cause I was scared Mommy would find out what I put in my purse. She said, "Why are you so quiet?"

I didn't know what to say. She said, "Are you thinking about Grandpa?" I nodded. She said, "He'll be fine. Let's pray for him right now." So she prayed, and that helped me feel a little better.

Then I said, "Do you think Grandpa finished my song?" Mommy said, "Grandpa's knee hurts a lot. Don't ask him about the song today." So I said, "He wants to write a song for me so we can be snack buddies *and* song buddies." Mommy said, "Don't ask him about the song, Lori. Just let Grandpa get better."

When we got to his room, Grandma was there, and Grandpa was sitting up in bed, eating lunch. I whispered to Mommy, "We should close the door so Grandpa won't get in trouble for eating in bed." Mommy whispered, "It's OK. The hospital people brought him the food."

But he wasn't eating much of it. Maybe the food at the hospital isn't as good as the food Mommy fixes. She's smart. When she fixes food for me, she lets me choose. She says, "Do you want apple slices or orange slices for lunch?" Then I think about which one to choose instead of thinking about being a fussy eater.

And sometimes she gives me choices when we have a "magic lunch." A "magic lunch" is when Mommy makes sandwiches and cuts watermelon into thin slices. Then I say, "I'm going to turn my food into a Christmas tree or a star." And I do. I choose a cookie cutter and push it down on my food. It's fun to pretend I'm doing a magic trick and turning my sandwich or watermelon slice into a fun shape. I bet Grandpa would eat more if the hospital let him have a magic lunch.

I told Grandpa, "I have some good food for you." Then I opened my purse, and I pulled out the bread crusts I cut off and put in my purse when Mommy was on the phone. They were in a sandwich bag. I pulled them out of the bag and said, "These will help your knee get better, 'cause if eating crusts helps me run faster, they will help your knee so you can walk faster."

He got a tear in his eye, hugged me, and said, "Thank you. That's wonderful, with a capital W!" I know why he had a tear in his eye. He was happy 'cause he knew the bread crusts would help him get better. Then Mommy put the plastic sandwich bag in the waste trashket.

I wanted to ask Grandpa if he finished my song, but I didn't want to make Mommy mad, so I waited till she left the room to talk to a nurse. She took you with her. After she left, I asked, "Grandpa, did you finish your song for me?" Grandpa said, "No, my knee hurts so much I haven't been able to think about it."

When Mommy came back in the room, she asked Grandpa, "Did you sleep well last night?" He said, "No, I had a lot of trouble falling asleep." I used to be crabby about going to bed, too, but not anymore. 'Cause at our house, just before bedtime, the Bedtime Elf sneaks in my room and puts two of our toys and two of our books under my pillow. After I have my snack and get my pajamas on, I go in my room and look under the pillow. It's a fun surprise every night. I know the Bedtime Elf is really Mommy, but it's fun to pretend. I bet Grandpa would sleep better if the hospital had a Bedtime Elf.

Anyway, that was our visit at the hospital last week. Now it's Tuesday again. Grandpa's knee is doing a lot better. He stayed home tonight, and that's why we just have Grandma tonight. But Grandpa will come over next Tuesday 'cause Grandma said Grandpa's knee is feeling a lot better. I told her, "I think the crusts are helping him."

I guess Grandpa's knee is going to be OK. But now I'm worried about something else. I'm scared Grandpa won't work on my song while his knee is getting better. And by the time it's all better, he might forget about my song.

TAKE-AWAY VALUE

Think About It

In this chapter, Lori explains the enjoyable bedtime routine at her house, involving the Bedtime Elf. Routines can be a positive experience that parents and kids like. If you're skeptical, think of birthday and holiday traditions that kids enjoy.

Create a positive bedtime routine which has a predictable sequence of events that culminates in your youngster going to sleep. If the elements of the routine are positive, your child will be more cooperative about going to bed.

Here are three suggestions. First, include activities your child enjoys. Second, keep it mellow. It's a good time for songs and stories, but a bad time for playing tag with Daddy. Third, vary the routine as needed in order to maintain the child's interest. If you've been reading stories every night, play a game, or let your child draw pictures.

Talk About It

1. What are some of your favorite rituals or routines throughout the course of a year?
2. What makes those routines enjoyable?
3. Describe your child's current bedtime routine.
4. Brainstorm what new elements you could put into the bedtime routine.

Try It

Try the revised bedtime routine with your child.

Chapter 24

When Grandma Reads to Me

Tuesday, August 10th

GRANDMA'S HERE! AND Grandpa's here, too! He's still on crutches, but he's here. It's funner when they're both here.

When they pulled up in our driveway, I jumped up and down like a bunny rabbit. Then I ran around the living room and hollered, "Grandma and Grandpa are here! Grandma and Grandpa are here!" I hope they come over every Tuesday for the rest of my life! Right now, they're talking to Mommy and Daddy. That's why I can talk to you now.

Grandma brought a bag of books from the library where she works. She always brings books to read to us. My favorite book is *Cinderella.*[7] But some stuff in the book isn't right, 'cause it's not the same as the movie.

I love it when she reads to us 'cause she's real good at it. She knows how to change her voice when the people are talking and stuff. I think she learned how to read like that from working in the library.

One time, Grandma was reading *Little Bear* to me.[8] Teddy Bear listened too, 'cause he likes books about bears. But I told him to move, 'cause I couldn't see the pictures. After we finished the story, Grandpa came into the living room and sat by himself on the other side of the room. So I walked over and said, "Grandpa, you can hold Teddy Bear, so you won't be lonely." Grandpa smiled and said, "Thank you very much."

Then Grandpa whispered in Teddy Bear's ear. I said, "What did you say to Teddy Bear?" Grandpa said, "I asked him if he liked the story, but he didn't answer me." I told Grandpa, "That's 'cause he only talks to me."

Anyway, I love stories 'cause they're fun, and they help me feel better too. I have lots of feelings, and sometime my feelings are big and scary.

Real scary. They're the boss of me, and I can't help myself very much. But when I listen to a story about somebody else who got scared, and their story turns out OK, then I know I don't have to be scared about what might happen to me.

Grandma brings all kinds of books on stuff I like. One time she brought a book from the library about a teddy bear that got lost. But don't worry, Tommy, they found him again, just like we found Rascal. Lots of times Grandma reads us Bible stories. They're interesting, the pictures are cool, and I sit on her lap when she reads to me. I love it when she reads to me.

Anyway, I wonder what books Grandma brought today. I hope she brought a story about snakes, 'cause we went to the St. Louis Zoo on Saturday. I liked the snakes, Mommy liked the baby giraffe, and Daddy liked that we got into the zoo for free.

At first, I was scared of the snakes, but Mommy said, "They can't get you, and they're interesting, because if they get cold, they can't make their bodies warmer. They need help, and they have to move next to a warm rock to get warmer." That's how us kids are with our feelings, Tommy. We need help to change how we feel. So we love fun toys and playing with friends 'cause those things help us feel good.

And we complain when playtime is over or when we have to leave a friend's house, 'cause we don't know how to be happy then. It's like taking a snake away from the rock that was nice and warm.

But a lot of grown-ups don't know this, so they get mad at their kids and say, "You had a long time to play in the park. Don't complain." But when Sarah's Mommy takes us to the park, she says, "Sarah and Lori, playtime is over, and it's time to go to the car." Then she gets a sneaky look on her face and says, "I bet I can beat you to the car!" She runs, but we do too, and we always beat her. And we're not crabby since we're thinking about how much fun it is to race.

Mommy is the same way. When I have to stop playing, she helps me think about something else. She'll say, "It's time to get ready for bed. What do you want for snack? And what do you think the Bedtime Elf will bring tonight?"

Another good thing is when they read us stories. Stories are good 'cause they help us with our feelings. That's why I like to have the same story read over and over to me. Asking to hear the same good story over and over is like a cold snake that keeps going back to the rock that's always warm.

Anyway, I hope Grandma brought a story about snakes and a book about a race 'cause the neighborhood party is in two weeks. At the party, there's going to be a race, and I'm going to beat Jimmy Brodnick! Then he'll have to stop being mean. I'm pretty fast now 'cause I've been running a lot and eating my crusts.

And next week, I almost forgot to tell you, we have Vacation Bible School. It's like Sunday school, but it's every day. I'll be with my friends and not have to worry about seeing Jimmy Brodnick. Mommy said we'll sing songs, make stuff, and hear Bible stories. I love Bible stories, Tommy! Our teacher probably won't be as good at telling stories as Grandma, but she can't help it. She's not a grandma yet.

Anyway, I love having story time with Grandma, and she likes it, too. I know she does 'cause one time, I was sitting on her lap while she read me *Cinderella*. After the story, she hugged me and said, "Lori, I love reading to you and having you on my lap. But you're getting big, and pretty soon we won't be able to snuggle like this anymore." I thought hard and figgered it out. I hugged her and said, "Don't worry, Grandma. Maybe God will grow me smaller."

TAKE-AWAY VALUE

Think About It

Preschoolers are ruled by their feelings. But listening to stories helps kids learn to manage their emotions. Stories provide a safe way for kids to experience and work through feelings because they often identify with the characters.

Most children's stories offer a message of reassurance that despite difficulty, the child can make it through tough times. For example, in *A Grace Disguised*,[9] Gerald Sittser relates that after his wife died, his son loved *Bambi*.[10] The youngster realized that like himself, Bambi lost his mother. He also noted that Bambi grew up to be king of the forest. Another example involves a preschooler I know who was separated from his mother for nearly a month and missed her greatly. During that separation, he watched the movie *Dumbo*[11] every day.

How can you find time to read to your kids? First, ask for help. Recruit your spouse, the grandparents, a babysitter, and older siblings to read to your preschooler. Second, get a fresh set of books from the library. Having different books relieves the tedium of reading the same story repeatedly . Third, see if your library offers recorded books for young children. If so, buy a cheap CD or cassette player so your child can listen to a recorded book while looking at the pictures and turning pages along with the story.

Talk About It

1. If you needed surgery and a friend who'd had the same operation explained what helped her get through it, how would you feel? That's similar to the encouragement stories give children.
2. What is your child's favorite story?
3. What strategies have you used to include stories in your child's schedule?
4. What's the biggest obstacle that interferes with reading stories to your child? How could you overcome the obstacle?

Try It

Read a story to your child today.

Chapter 25

Guess Who

Tuesday, August 17th

TOMMY! TOMMY! GUESS who came to Vacation Bible School today. JIMMY BRODNICK! I couldn't believe it! So I watched him real close the whole entire time. And it's a good thing I did.

Vacation Bible School is like Sunday school, except we have it every day this week. We do Bible stories, songs, crafts, and get a snack. It was fun yesterday, but not today with Jimmy there!

Anyway, we were in Mrs. Watson's class. I sat next to Sarah, and Jimmy sat across the table from me. When the Bible story started, Jimmy waited until the teacher wasn't looking, and then he stuck his tongue out at me. And when Mrs. Watson turned away from us to pick up a picture off her desk, he showed his teeth at me, like Rascal does when she's mad at the mailman. Then he whispered, "Girls are dumb." But the teacher didn't hear.

So I said, "Mrs. Watson? Jimmy said, 'Girls are dumb.'" Mrs. Watson looked at Jimmy and said, "Jimmy, tell me what happened between you and Lori." He said, "I didn't say anything. Honest." And he smiled at her. She said, "It's important for all of us to talk nicely to each other."

Then she turned around to pick up another picture off her desk for the Bible story, but she turned back to the class real fast, and this time she caught Jimmy calling me "stupid." She said, "Jimmy, I saw what you said. You need to go to the corner and sit in the time-out chair."

She said it just like Mommy does when she gives me a time-out. Mrs. Watson didn't holler. She was real calm and told Jimmy, "Since you're five years old, I'll set the timer for five minutes. Don't ask me if your time is up yet. You'll know it's done when the timer beeps." Mommy does that too. She used to be on the phone and would forget to tell me my time-out was over, so I'd holler from my time-out chair to ask if I could get up, and Mommy would holler back that I'm supposed to be quiet in time-out. But now she uses the timer, and we don't shout during time-outs anymore.

When Jimmy's time-out was over, he came back to the table, and Mrs. Watson switched him to a chair right by her. He didn't call me names when we were sitting at the table. But when we lined up to get a drink and use the bathroom, he tried to kick me, but he missed. Mrs. Watson saw that, and made Jimmy go to the back of the line. After we got our drink, we went to the playground. Mrs. Watson set the timer, and Jimmy had to take a time-out for the first part of the playground time. Why did he have to come and ruin everything? Vacation Bible School was great until Jimmy came.

Mrs. Watson is an awesome teacher. She tells Bible stories real good, and she has a marble jar on her desk. When we're being good, she lets us put a marble in the jar. When the marble jar gets full, the whole class gets a treat or extra time on the playground.

Yesterday, I got to put two marbles in. One time it was 'cause I was listening extra good. And another time, I shared my crayons with a girl, and Mrs. Watson said, "That was very nice, Lori. You may put a marble in the jar." It's easy to listen and be nice when the teacher makes it fun.

When we got back to our room after being on the playground, we prayed. Mrs. Watson had her eyes closed, but she had her hand on Jimmy's shoulder so he couldn't do anything bad. Guess what Jimmy did. He had his eyes open the whole entire time! It's called being a "peeking Tom."

On the way home, I told Mommy, "Jimmy had his eyes open the whole time we prayed." Mommy said, "How do you know his eyes were open? Were your eyes open too?" I told her, "Sometimes, you have to peek to make sure other people aren't peeking." And I told Mommy about the mean things Jimmy did.

Mommy said, "I'll talk to Mrs. Brodnick and Mrs. Watson about what Jimmy did. But even though it's hard, Jesus told us to love our neighbor." Mommy put her arm around me and said, "Loving our neighbor means we're supposed to love everybody, especially the ones who are hardest to love. And Jesus wants us to pray for them. When somebody is mean, there's usually something bothering them. That means they need God's help and our prayers." So Mommy prayed for Jimmy.

I asked Mommy, "But why did Jimmy have to come to Vacation Bible School?" Mommy said, "At Vacation Bible School, kids learn about Jesus, and everybody needs Jesus." I said, "I know everyone needs Jesus, but we don't need Jimmy." Then Mommy said, "In the Bible, there was a man named Saul who was mean to Christians. But he became a Christian, and if God could save him, he could save anybody." I guess Mommy's right, but I bet Saul never said, "Girls are dumb" or tried to kick them and stuff. Then Mommy asked me, "Do you have any questions?" I said, "No. Can we stop talking about this stuff so I can play?" She said, "Yes."

After I played for a while, Mommy talked to me again. She said, "I called Mrs. Watson. She'll have Jimmy sit by her, and she'll watch him real closely. I also called Mrs. Brodnick and told her what Jimmy did. She'll have a talk with Jimmy."

We don't have Vacation Bible School next week, but the neighborhood picnic is on Tuesday. You know what that means, don't you, Tommy? We're going to have lots of food, a clown, and most of all, there's going to be a kids' race. I'm going to beat Jimmy Brodnick, and he's going to have to stop being mean to me and saying girls are dumb. You'll see.

TAKE-AWAY VALUE

Think About It

Time-outs serve as a good discipline strategy because they go to the root of a child's misbehavior. Young children frequently get stuck in their feelings. When they get stuck in crabby feelings, their behavior turns negative.

But a time-out takes the child out of the immediate situation where the bad behavior occurred. By doing so, it lets the child step back from the situation and get "unstuck" from the crabby feelings.

Here are three suggestions for time-outs. First, give the time-out calmly. Venting your anger delays the process of the child regaining self-control. Second, set a timer for one minute per year of the child's age. A three-year-old gets a three-minute time-out and a five-year-old gets a five-minute time-out. Third, walk away after you give the time-out. This makes further complaints from your child less likely.

Talk About It

1. When were you stuck in negative feelings? What changed your mood?
2. When was your youngster stuck in negative feelings? What changed his or her mood?
3. Do you give time-outs? Why or why not?
4. Proper use of time-outs allows more time for positive interaction with your youngster. What enjoyable activities would you like to do more often with your preschooler?

Try It

Use the ideas above to give your child a time-out.

Chapter 26

The Race

Tuesday, August 24th

TOMMY! ...TOMMY!...DID YOU see me? It was...the race! Whew! It's hard...to catch...my breath. I was waiting... for this race...for a long time.

It's Tuesday evening, and Grandma and Grandpa are here, but Mommy and Daddy are here too 'cause we're having the neighborhood party and the race. Remember?

Anyway, I just did my race. Right before the race, Grandpa told me, "You have to run the whole length of the block, so don't run your fastest. Run medium fast, so you won't get tired out too soon. The other kids will run real fast at first, but then they'll get tired, and you'll pass them. Run medium fast." He hugged me and said, "Have fun! And I'm proud of you!"

Then it was time to line up for the race. My heart was going *thumpy-thumpy* and my hands were sweaty. We lined up at the starting line in the street, and I stood next to Sarah. I liked having my best friend next to me for the most important race of my whole entire life.

When I turned my head away from Sarah, there was Jimmy Brodnick on the other side of me! The man in charge of the race was talking into a microphone. I think he was telling us what to do, but I couldn't hear him 'cause Jimmy was talking. He said, "Your shoes are old and dumb. My parents got me some brand-new gym shoes that will make me go super fast. But you're going to run real slow 'cause you're a dumb girl with dumb shoes, and because boys are way better than girls."

Then Mommy hollered, "Good luck, Lori!" and I looked to see where she was. When I looked for her, I felt something pull on my shoelace. I looked down and saw that Jimmy had untied one of my shoes. Right then, the man in charge blew a whistle. All the kids started running, and the parents were cheering. I didn't know the whistle was the signal to start, so I didn't start running right away. Everyone else took off and got ahead of me, and Jimmy was *way* ahead of me.

I started, and I tried to run medium fast, like Grandpa said, but my shoelace was untied. I worried, "What if my shoe falls off?" I felt the shoe laces going "flip, flop, flip, flop" back and forth across my shoe while I ran. Jimmy was so far ahead I didn't know how I could ever catch up. I thought, "Maybe Jimmy's shoes are helping him run way faster than me."

But I decided to trust what Grandpa said more than what Jimmy said. And I thought about what Mommy told me one time. She said, "Don't listen to what bad people say. Listen to what good people say and what the Bible says. When we listen to the wrong people, we think the wrong things. And when we think the wrong things, we do the wrong things." So I decided to think about what Grandpa said, not what Jimmy said. And I ran medium fast.

But my shoelaces were flopping even more. And every couple of steps, my shoe got looser. It felt like it was starting to fall off my foot. And that's not all. My legs got real tired, and I was breathing hard. I didn't think the race would be this hard. But right then, Grandpa hollered, "It's working, Lori! Medium fast! You're gaining on him!" I looked, and he was right! I was about halfway down the block, passing in front of our house. Jimmy was only about one house ahead of me, and I had caught up with Sarah.

Jimmy was slowing down, but my shoe was almost off. I didn't know what to do. Would Mommy be mad if I lost my shoe? She gets upset when I lose my stuff. But I kept running medium fast.

Then I caught up with Jimmy! He looked at me and said, "Ha, ha... your dumb shoe...is falling off...And then...you won't be able...to run." Then I heard Grandpa holler, "Keep running! Medium fast!" So I did what Grandpa told me to do. But I thought, "What if Jimmy's right. What if my shoe falls off?"

We were past Sarah's house now, and had only four houses to go to the finish of the race. That's when I passed Jimmy. Then I got scared of something else. What if he ran up close behind me and pulled my hair real hard? I got real nervous, and I guess I slowed down thinking about it, 'cause Jimmy passed me, with only two houses to go. Two houses to go, and then the race would be over at the end of the block. And if Jimmy beat me, he'd keep being mean!

Then I saw the big sign at the end of the race—the sign for The Firehouse Restaurant. I couldn't read the words, but I recognized it 'cause they have the same sign at the restaurant. I decided there was no way I was going to let Jimmy get to the sign for *my* favorite restaurant before I did. I ran a little faster, and I caught up with Jimmy, with one house to go. I saw a bright yellow line of chalk on the street marking the end of the race and a bunch of parents behind it, cheering. Then I passed Jimmy, ran across the line, and won! I won! Some other kids finished ahead of me, but I still won 'cause I beat Jimmy Brodnick!

Mommy hugged me and said, "I'm proud of you, Lori. You worked very hard, and you ran a good race." Grandpa said, "That was wonderful. With a capital W!"

I was so tired and so happy all at the same time. Don't worry, little brother. When you learn to walk, I'll teach you to run like this, too. You have to practice. You have to eat your crusts. You have to listen to the right people. And you have to run medium fast.

TAKE-AWAY VALUE

Think About It

Lori's grandfather told her to run medium fast. This helped because like most youngsters, Lori couldn't fully understand what a new situation would be like. As a result, preschoolers don't know what to say or do in new situations. Offering a clear suggestion helps like handing them a flashlight at night helps them find their way through an unfamiliar territory.

This is important for big life changes such as when you move or when the child's parents divorce. But it's also important for smaller events that are new to them. Some examples might be attending a wedding, going to the dentist, or making friends with the new neighbor.

Tell your child, "On Saturday, a new family is moving in next door. When you meet the kids, tell them your name, and ask them what their names are." Say, "In a couple of days, we're going to Uncle Doug's wedding. We'll be dressed up, and we'll sit quietly and watch, like we do during church."

Talk About It

1. What was a challenging new experience that happened to you as an adult?
2. Did anyone help prepare you for it? If so, how did you feel? If not, how did you feel about having to figure it out on your own?
3. How do your kids respond to new experiences? Give examples.
4. How do you prepare them for new experiences? Give examples.

Try It

Talk to your child about an upcoming new experience.

Chapter 27

The Gift

Tuesday, August 31st

WHEN GRANDMA AND Grandpa came over tonight, Grandpa said hi, and went right down to the basement. I asked Grandma, "What's Grandpa doing?" She said, "You'll find out in a little bit." So I played school with Grandma. She was the teacher, I was the good kid, and Rascal was the naughty kid.

I know all about school. You learn stuff, like the three "R's"—readin', 'ritin', and recess. And you learn other stuff too, like

> Thirty days has September,
> April, June, and...I can't remember.

Sometimes school is hard, but don't quit. You have to stay in school and finish your vegetation! And when you're at school, don't be mean, like Jimmy Brodnick was to me at Vacation Bible School.

I told you I'd beat him, and then he'd have to stop being mean to me and saying boys are better than girls. I was right! I beat him in the race, and now he has to go to kinny garden all day, so he's not here to be mean. And I'm going to school this year, too. Next week, I start preschool for two mornings a week.

After we finished playing school, Grandpa came into the room and said, "Lori, I want to tell you something and give you something." I said, "What is it?" He said, "First, I am going to tell you something. Grandma and I have enjoyed coming over every Tuesday. It's been fun to play with you and Tommy."

He got quiet and stared at the floor. Then he said, "But I'm teaching at a different school this year, and it's a lot of work." Grandma and I won't be coming over every Tuesday. I need more time to get my teaching lessons ready. We'll still see you a lot, but not every Tuesday."

I cried, and I squeaked, "Nooo! I want you to come over every Tuesday 'cause that makes it the best day of the week. You *have* to." I cried harder, and Grandpa hugged me.

When our hug was done, Grandpa said, "There's another reason we're making this change. Your parents want to start having family night. Twice a month, on Tuesday evenings, you and your brother will do some fun things with your parents. Your Mommy and Daddy said I could tell you about family night because it's one of the reasons Grandma and I won't come over on Tuesday nights." He was quiet for a little bit, and he said, "You'll like family night. You'll play games, and you'll get to do fun things." I stopped crying, and I wasn't feeling so sad.

Grandpa said, "That is what I wanted to tell you. Now I have something to give you." I asked, "Where is it? Can I open it?" He said, "It's not that kind of gift. I wrote a song for you. It's about Teddy Bear. A couple of weeks ago, on a Tuesday night, I came in to check on you after you went to bed. You were asleep, but Teddy Bear was awake."

I asked, "What did you do?" Grandpa said, "I asked Teddy if he could keep a secret, and he nodded his head. I told him I was going to write a song for you, and I asked him if he wanted to help me write it."

I asked Grandpa, "Did he?" Grandpa said, "Teddy Bear smiled, but he didn't say anything." So I told Grandpa, "That's 'cause Teddy only talks to me." Grandpa said, "I asked Teddy if he loves you, and he nodded his head. And I told Teddy that I love you and Tommy, too. And Teddy smiled again." Then I hugged Teddy Bear and looked at him to see what he would say. But he was so happy he couldn't talk.

Then Grandpa went into the basement, came back with his guitar, and sang me the song. When he finished, I clapped and said, "Sing it again! Sing it again!" So he did. Then I shouted, "Grandpa, Grandpa! This means we're song buddies!" He smiled and said, "Yes. It feels good to be song buddies with you, Lori." Don't worry Tommy, I bet Grandpa will write a song for you so you can be song buddies, too.

Then he gave me a copy of the song on a CD. He recorded it on his friend's computer. So I'm going to put the CD in the CD player that Mommy and Daddy keep in your room to play lullabies on. I'm turning it on now. Listen, Tommy. Here's the song:

Mommy puts me to bed. She tucks me in.
She pulls all the covers up to my chin.
She kisses me and says "Good-night."
She gives me Teddy Bear and turns out the light.
Then in the darkness, I see shadows ...faces...of animals... monsters...
I think they want to get me.
I start to be afraid, but Teddy won't let me.
He says, "They're all OK."
He says, "They've come to play."

> How you care, how you care, Teddy Bear.
> You are there when I need you.
> How you care, how you care, Teddy Bear.
> Oh, I love you, Teddy Bear.

There are times when I'm sick; I can't go out to play.
I have to stay on my bed and just rest up all day.
I'm feverish and get the chills.
My parents make me take all those icky little pills.
And when I lie there I feel tired, lonely, really sad,
Wishing that someone would play with me.
I look at Teddy Bear, and he says he will stay with me.
He says, "I'll be your friend." And then he says,
"Let's play pretend!"

> How you care, how you care, Teddy Bear.
> You are there, when I need you.
> How you care, how you care, Teddy Bear.
> Oh, I love you, Teddy Bear .

Anyway, after Grandpa sang the song twice, I hugged him, climbed up on his lap, and asked him, "Will you still visit us?" He said, "You bet." I asked him, "Are we still snack buddies?" He said, "You bet." I asked him, "Are we still song buddies?" He said, "You bet."

Then he asked me, "Will you take good care of your brother?" I said, "You bet." He asked, "Will you still draw pictures for me?" I said, "You bet." He asked, "Will you still be a good girl for Grandma and me?" I put my arms around his neck, hugged him tight, and said, "You bet! With a capital W!"

TAKE-AWAY VALUE

Think About It

Grandpa knew Lori would be upset when she learned that her grandparents wouldn't be coming over every Tuesday. He wisely took time to talk to Lori and offer encouragement and affection. Take a similar approach with your preschooler.

Your child's sorrow and fear are open doors. Walk through them to touch his or her heart. Do this by offering sympathy in the way you listen and what you say. Don't be too quick to tell your child the situation will be all right.

In addition to offering comfort, Grandpa gave Lori something tangible—a song. You may not be able to write a song, but you can offer something concrete. Here are four examples. First, draw a picture on the back of your son's hand the night before his first day at a new preschool. It's a physical reminder of your love, and he can't lose it. Second, if you or your spouse goes away on a business trip, buy matching T-shirts to use as pajama shirts. Give one to your preschooler and the other to the parent who's going out of town. The child will feel a link to the travelling parent who is wearing a matching T-shirt to bed. Third, if a child expresses fears when going to bed, provide a night-light or stuffed animal. Fourth, before you move, offer a photograph of the park that's near the new home.

Talk About It

1. As an adult, when were you sad or afraid? Who listened and talked with you sympathetically? How did you feel toward that person?
2. What makes it difficult to reach out to your child emotionally when he or she is afraid or sad? Examples might include being in a hurry, tired, or upset with the child for something he or she did earlier in the day.
3. How will your child feel when you reach out to him or her emotionally?
4. What effect will that have on your relationship with him or her?

Try It

The next time your child is sad or afraid, use it as an opportunity to connect with your child in a powerful way.

Endnotes

1. Dan Allender, *How Children Raise Parents*, Colorado Springs, CO: Waterbrook Press, 1996, p. 9.
2. Brian Jacques, *The Bellmaker*, New York: Ace Books, 1996, p. 339.
3. *The Holy Bible*. New International Version. Grand Rapids, MI: Zondervan, 1978 .
4. Peter DeVries, *The Tunnel of Love*, Boston: Little and Company, 1954, p. 97, 98.
5. Thomas Phelan, *1, 2, 3 Magic: Effective Discipline for Children 2-12*, Glen Ellyn, IL: ParentMagic, 2003.
6. *Cinderella*, DVD, Brandy Norwood, Bernadette Peters, Robert Iscove, Walt Disney Video: Burbank, CA: 2003.
7. R.H. Disney, *Walt Disney's Cinderella*, New York: Random House, 2005.
8. Elsa Holmelund Minarik, *Little Bear*, New York: Harper Collins, 1985.
9. Gerald Sittser, *A Grace Disguised*, Grand Rapids, MI: Zondervan, 1995
10. Felix Salten, *Bambi,* New York: Golden Books, an imprint of Random House, 2004.
11. *Dumbo,* DVD, A.Kendall O'Connor, Al Zinnen, Bill Roberts, Walt Disney Home Entertainment: Burbank, CA: 2006.

Deleted Scenes

Below you'll find some deleted scenes, like at the end of a DVD. Some provide parenting tips or insight. Other selections offer humor. These are all in Lori's words.

Today I punched a pillow. Mommy asked, "What are you doing?" I told her, "The pillow is Jimmy Brodnick, and I'm hitting him 'cause he's mean." She said, "Don't do that. You should be nice to other people, and if they're still mean to you, tell a grown-up." So I stopped punching the pillow. A little later, Mommy saw me hitting a couch cushion. I told her, "This is a different game. I'm pretending the cushion is a snake that's trying to bite Daddy. So I'm hitting the snake. And it's extra fun 'cause the snake's name is 'Jimmy Brodnick.'" She said, "You need to find a different game."

Somebody told Daddy that turning on a vacuum cleaner makes a fussy baby stop crying. So when you cry and cry, Tommy, Daddy vacuums the living room, and you get quiet right away.

Daddy says Mommy believes in "NCLB." That stands for "No Coffee Left Behind."

Grandma and Grandpa are coming over tonight. Grandma is the one who brings us books from the library, and Grandpa is the one with bald hair.

Grandpa's hair is gray but Grandma's isn't. She told me, "I use a little coloring in my hair. A lot of grandmas do that." Then I figgered it out.

When people get older, their hair turns gray, and it falls out. It's like dandelion seeds that turn gray and fall off. But grandmas color their hair to keep it from turning gray, and that keeps their hair from falling out. But grandpas don't color their hair, so they lose it. Somebody should tell the grandpas.

Grandpa plays checkers with me. But he's not very good at it, 'cause I always win.

Grown-ups don't understand why we don't like going to bed. Here's why. Grown-ups work all day at their jobs or around the house. After supper they do dishes and mow the lawn and stuff. They like going to bed 'cause it means they get to stop working. But us kids play all day, and we hate going to bed 'cause it means we have to stop playing.

God told Noah to build a big boat 'cause of the flood. After the flood, God sent a rainbow to say he'd never send a flood like that. The rainbow's name is the St. Louis Arch.

We had fun today when Mommy couldn't find the cordless phone, the part you talk into. So she pushed the button on the part that plugs into the wall. The missing part went, "*NEE-NOO, NEE-NOO, NEE-NOO*." We raced to see who could find it first. I won 'cause I found it first. I said, "Do that again!" This time I hid the phone. When Mommy pushed the button to make it go, "NEE-NOO," we took off looking for it. I found it before Mommy. I guess I'm just better at that game than she is.

Mommy gave someone a suggestion. She laughed and said, "My spiritual gift is thinking up work for *other* people to do." She said, "It's the gift that keeps on giving."

Yesterday I asked Mommy, "May I have a cookie?" She said, "No." Then I lied. I said, "But you promised me a cookie!" Mommy said, "No I didn't." But I cried, and she let me have a cookie, 'cause parents hate breaking promises to their kids.

But then Mommy made a "Promise Sheet." If she promises me something, I have to ask her to write it on the Promise Sheet, and then she'll write it down. Today I told her she promised me a cookie, and I cried. But she said, "It's not on the Promise Sheet." So she didn't have to give me a cookie. Sometimes it's no fun having a smart Mommy.

Mommy's sneaky. If she wants me to take a bath, she says, "Do you want your bath now or in fifteen minutes?" Instead of thinking about whether or not I'll obey, I think about when to take my bath. If I say, "I don't want to take a bath!" Mommy calmly says, "You have a choice. You may take it now or in fifteen minutes, or I can decide. Will you pick the time or will I?" Then I say, "Sheesh! I'll take my bath in fifteen minutes."

Grown-ups always say they're different from us kids, but I'm not so sure. Little kids drink from a sippy cup that has a hole in the cover. Mommy has a sippy cup too. It's tall and silvery with a hole in the top so she can drink her coffee.

Grandpa says, "Let your conscience be your TV Guide."

Daddy was watching the weather report on TV, and I asked him, "What's a media urologist?" He laughed but didn't tell me. I don't think he knows.

Recommended Resources

1. Focus on the Family is a Christian organization that offers radio programs, publications, and a Web site to equip individuals for many aspects of family life, including child rearing. Their Web site is www.focusonthefamily.org.
2. Hearts at Home (www.hearts-at-home.org) is a Christ-centered organization that encourages, educates, and equips women in the profession of motherhood. They offer conferences, publications, and more.
3. Mothers of Preschoolers (MOPS) focuses on the interests and needs of mothers with children from infancy through kindergarten. It is a Christian organization that offers conferences, publications, and local groups for mothers. To learn more or to find a local MOPS group, visit their Web site: www.mops.org.
4. At www.aap.org, the American Academy of Pediatrics offers authoritative advice for children from birth through age twenty-one.
5. *1-2-3 Magic: Effective Discipline for Children 2-12* by Dr. Tom Phelan gives clear and practical advice on the subject of discipline. In addition to the book, his Web site offers a free newsletter and other resources. The Web site is www.parentmagic.com.
6. Judy Rogers has recorded Christian songs for families with children. Her child-oriented albums are *Why Can't I See God?*, *Go to the Ant*, *Guard Your Heart*, and *Teach Me While My Heart is Tender*. For more information, visit www.judyrogers.com.

Ten Quick Tips for Parents of Preschoolers

1. Play with your child.
2. Make your first words of the day to your preschooler positive words.
3. Shorten your to-do list so you have more time to enjoy your kids.
4. Pray with your child.
5. Cultivate a positive relationship with your spouse. If you're divorced, make the relationship as peaceful as possible.
6. Take your child to church with you.
7. Laugh with your preschooler.
8. Nurture relationships with adults who relate well to your youngster.
9. Read to your child.
10. Hire a babysitter occasionally, so you can have a break.

Ten Quick Tips for Grandparents of Preschoolers

1. Offer to babysit.
2. Read to your grandchild.
3. Send a cute picture postcard.
4. Pray for your grandchild.
5. Center the conversation on your grandchild's interests.
6. Occasionally give fun, inexpensive gifts as a surprise.
7. Make a space in your home that's filled with things your grandchild can play with, even if it's only a few drawers or shelves.
8. Arrange for one-on-one time with your grandchild.
9. Be a good listener.
10. Respect the way your son or daughter disciplines your grandchild.

Author Interview

Q: Why did you write the book from a child's perspective?

A: I wanted to help adults understand how kids think. The best way to do that is to take adults inside a child's mind.

Q: Was Lori modeled after a particular child?

A: No. I drew ideas for her personality and thinking from many different children.

Q: How long did it take to write the book?

A: I worked on it off and on for ten years. I've worked on it steadily for the past five years.

Q: Lori says grown-ups don't remember what it felt like to be a preschooler. How did you overcome that barrier?

A: I watched how veteran preschool teachers connected with kids. I also watched the kids closely. When you are in a room of ten preschool children, the patterns in their behavior and reasoning become more apparent than when you're with one or two preschoolers in your own home.

Q: Did your experiences as a parent help you write this book?

A: Yes. I started writing this book when our sons were young. Some of the strategies Lori suggests were things I discovered through parenting. But I drew ideas from many different children and from many different parents and grandparents.

Q: **Why did you write about preschoolers?**

A: Working at preschools, I was fascinated by the strategies the experienced teachers used to connect with the children.

Q: **What do you enjoy most about preschoolers?**

A: They have amazing imaginations. One day they'll pretend to explore the jungle. A few hours later, they're imagining they're piloting a spaceship on its way to Mars.

Q: **Why did you place the book in St. Louis?**

A: I enjoyed living there. I earned my Ph.D. at St. Louis University, met and married my wife there, and worked in a preschool there.

Q: **What do you think is the single best piece of advice for the parent or grandparent of a preschooler?**

A: Watch and listen to your child or grandchild to discover his or her needs. Be ready to change the way you relate to them in order to meet those needs.

You May Have a Preschooler if...

1. Your child has to go to the bathroom the moment you get his or her snowsuit on.
2. Your windows have more fingerprints than an FBI crime lab.
3. Your bathtub has more toys than soap.
4. The stuffed animals in your house have names.
5. You hear the word *why* one hundred times a day.
6. You get a fistful of dandelions as a bouquet.
7. You look forward to going to the bathroom unaccompanied.
8. You know the location of all the local fast food restaurants with a play area.
9. You turn your head when a child says, "Mommy!" or "Daddy!" even though your youngster isn't in the room.
10. You've yelped after stepping on a Lego™ or Duplo™ in your stocking feet.

Topical Index

apology, ch. 12, 16
arguing, ch. 14, 21
asking why, (see questions)
bedtime, ch. 24
bedtime fears, ch. 8
car trips, ch. 4, 13
chores, ch. 10
eating (see fussy eaters)
excess energy, ch. 11
explaining what will happen, ch. 26
fear, ch. 2, 22, 27
feelings, ch. 5, 16, 27
fussy eaters, ch. 19, 23
gifts, ch. 12
imagination, ch. 16, 23
motivating good behavior, ch. 20, 21, 25
music, ch. 22
natural consequences, ch. 18
offer choices to gain compliance, ch. 23
play, ch. 4, 15
questions, ch. 6, 16
power of stories, ch. 24
read to your preschooler, ch. 24
sadness, ch. 7, 27
salvation, ch. 9
shopping, ch. 17
teaching your child, ch.12
thank you game, ch. 18
time-out, ch. 25
toys, ch. 4
vacation (see car trips)
when are we going to be there? (see car trips)
wiggles (see excess energy)
"yes rules", ch. 17

Also by Dr. Rob Currie, *Hungry for More of God*

You know the feeling. When mealtime is moments away, your mouth waters, your nose twitches, and your fingers fiddle with a fork. Just as we have an appetite for food, we also have a God-given hunger for intimacy with the Almighty. *Hungry for More of God* shows how to satisfy that hunger for deeper fellowship with God. The book includes questions after each chapter for individual or small group Bible study.

Responses to *Hungry for More of God*

In this excellent new work, Rob Currie uses a wonderful mixture of Scripture; engaging stories and quotations from the lives of noteworthy Christians; and insightful personal reflections in order to help whet your appetite and develop a deeper hunger for God. With *Hungry for More of God,* Rob has established himself as a spiritual author whose work is not to be missed!

ChristianBook.com

This is a spiritually insightful and solidly biblical book. One can't read this book without yearning to follow Christ more fully.

Illinois Baptist

Hungry for More of God is wonderful; spiritually and biblically solid; and the best book of its kind I've ever read! Plus it's entertaining and easy to read! If you're looking for an individual or group study book, I highly recommend it.

Mainstream

For those of us who know that we need more from God than we have—and don't know how to get it—this book is a gift that gives us hope.

Tony Campolo, Ph.D.
Eastern University

This book is an example of how to write a devotional text that challenges the mind and inspires the heart. Dr. Currie's writings have it all: alliteration, simile, word pictures, and above all, substance. His writing is clear, colorful, and compelling.

Church Libraries

***Hungry for More of God* is available online or through your local bookstore.**

Your Turn

Thank you for reading *Preschool Wisdom*. Please tell me what you liked about the book and what would have made it better. Send your comments to TheLoriBook@yahoo.com. Your feedback will help me write the sequel.

Contact Information

To order additional copies of this book, please visit
www.redemption-press.com.
Also available on Amazon.com and BarnesandNoble.com
Or by calling toll free 1-844-2REDEEM.

CPSIA information can be obtained
at www.ICGtesting.com
Printed in the USA
BVHW032108130122
626204BV00005B/97

9 781632 327420